Trees
Stages 1 & 2

A Unit for teachers

Published for the Schools Council by
Macdonald Educational, London and New York

© Schools Council Publications 1973

First impression 1973
Second impression (with amendments) 1975
Third impression 1977

ISBN 0 356 04347 9

Published by
Macdonald Educational
Holywell House
Worship Street
London EC2A 2EN

850 Seventh Avenue
New York 10019

The chief author of this book is:

Sheila Parker

The other members of the Science 5/13 team are:

Len Ennever	Project Director
Albert James	Deputy Project Director
Wynne Harlen	Evaluator
Don Radford	
Roy Richards	
Mary Horn	

Made and printed by Waterlow (Dunstable) Limited

General preface

'Science 5/13' is a project sponsored jointly by the Schools Council, the Nuffield Foundation and the Scottish Education Department, and based at the University of Bristol School of Education. It aims at helping teachers to help children between the ages of five and thirteen years to learn science through first-hand experience using a variety of methods.

The Project produces books that comprise Units dealing with subject areas in which children are likely to conduct investigations. Some of these Units are supported by books of background information. The Units are linked by objectives that the Project team hopes children will attain through their work. The aims of the Project are explained in a general guide for teachers called *With objectives in mind,* which contains the Project's guide to Objectives for children learning science, reprinted at the back of each Unit.

Acknowledgements

The Project is deeply grateful to its many friends: to the local education authorities who have helped us work in their areas, to those of their staff who, acting as area representatives, have borne the heavy brunt of administering our trials, and to the teachers, heads and wardens who have been generous without stint in working with their children on our materials. The books we have written drew substance from the work they did for us, and it was through their critical appraisal that our materials reached their present form. For guidance, we had our sponsors, our Consultative Committee and, for support, in all our working, the University of Bristol. To all of them we acknowledge our many debts: their help has been invaluable.

Metrication

This has given us a great deal to think about. We have been given much good advice by well-informed friends, and we have consulted many reports by learned bodies. Following the advice and the reports whenever possible we have expressed quantities in metric units with Imperial units afterwards in square brackets if it seemed useful to state them so.

There are, however, some cases to which the recommendations are difficult to apply. For instance we have difficulty with units such as miles per hour (which has statutory force in this country) and with Imperial units that are still in current use for common commodities and, as far as we know, liable to remain so for some time. In these cases we have tried to use our common sense and, in order to make statements that are both accurate and helpful to teachers, we have quoted Imperial measures followed by the appropriate metric equivalents in square brackets if it seemed sensible to give them.

Where we have quoted statements made by children, or given illustrations that are children's work, we have left unaltered the units in which the children worked—in any case some of these units were arbitrary.

Contents

1 Introduction to the Unit

Why a Unit on trees?

Man needs trees. A list of all the things in our environment that come directly or indirectly from trees would be legion and evidence of great material dependence. And this dependence is greater than many realise, for if all trees were suddenly removed from earth, the intricate machinery of ecological balance would be thrown out of gear and our continued existence threatened.

But there is more to trees than utilitarian value. They are vital elements in our visual landscape, which delight the seeing eye, and evoke aesthetic response.

Clearly, trees play an important part in the life of man, and this is a very good reason for including them in school work. But there is another, equally valid reason for their inclusion in classroom activity. They provide a ready source of material for observation and investigation which is likely to further the development of children's scientific understanding, and it is this aspect of trees that forms the substance of the Unit.

Using the Unit

There is no one 'right' way of using this Unit. Essentially, it is a source book for teachers. It contains suggestions for things children could do when working with trees and ideas about why they might do them.

The 'doing things' occur mainly in Chapters 4, 5 and 6. They are arranged under three seasonal headings because we thought this would be the most helpful framework for teachers operating within the time pattern of a school year. We suggest that you first browse through these activity chapters to get an over-all impression of possibilities, and subsequently dip into them as work develops.

The activity chapters are supported by Chapter 2 which considers ways of starting and developing work and Chapter 3 which considers some of the organisational points involved. These chapters are particularly relevant to teachers making a beginning with science work.

In the second part of Chapter 3 you will find most comment about what we hope children will achieve from their work and why we might encourage them in certain activities. The section links directly with another Project publication called *With objectives in mind* which sets out in detail the underlying philosophy of the Project. We recommend that you read this book during the course of your work and so appreciate how the Unit *Trees* relates to the Project as a whole. It has been developed not because we think that all children should necessarily have a better understanding of trees, but because we wanted to show how the subject matter of the Unit might be used to help develop their scientific understanding.

This, then, is the form of the Unit. We hope you will find in it material to select and adapt for your own class and will use it in ways that best suit your circumstances.

2 Finding profitable starting points

Any situation where children contact trees is a potential starting point. But whether or not it is a profitable one depends on positive answers to two questions:

Is it a situation that captures children's interest?

Is it one that could promote varied and sustained activities?

The first question can only be answered by individual teachers who know their children better than anyone else. The second, we shall illustrate by taking fairly obvious starting points and showing ways in which they might be developed.

Explore a playground tree

Choose a time when something interesting is happening. Seasonal events are useful:

Has anyone noticed the first flower, the first falling leaf, the first fruit?

Has anyone noticed its frost patterns?

Less obvious things are often more profitable.

Who has seen the spider's eggs in the bark?

Has anyone noticed the holes in some of the leaves?

Who has noticed the odd-coloured puddle collecting in the lowest branch? Is there anything in it?

Events of this kind promote discussion and serve to steer interest towards trees which children pass daily as

part of the general scene without registering them as things worth exploring.

Let us take one of the observations as an example and consider how it might be developed.

Flow chart 1

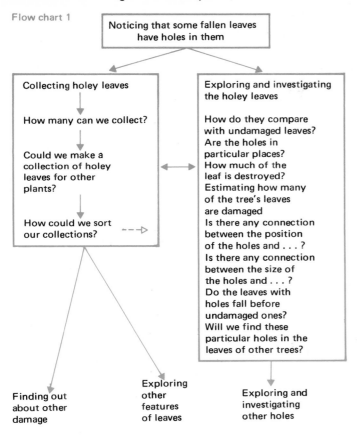

Noticing that some fallen leaves have holes in them

Collecting holey leaves

How many can we collect?

Could we make a collection of holey leaves for other plants?

How could we sort our collections?

Exploring and investigating the holey leaves

How do they compare with undamaged leaves? Are the holes in particular places? How much of the leaf is destroyed? Estimating how many of the tree's leaves are damaged Is there any connection between the position of the holes and . . . ? Is there any connection between the size of the holes and . . . ? Do the leaves with holes fall before undamaged ones? Will we find these particular holes in the leaves of other trees?

Finding out about other damage

Exploring other features of leaves

Exploring and investigating other holes

Make use of seasonal things

Seasonal 'bits and pieces' are an integral part of a country school's year, and in urban areas children can be encouraged to bring in things from parks and gardens. Any item needs discussion time to establish leads for exploratory work. Suppose, for example, someone brings sycamore fruits to school. How might the situation be developed? Flow chart 2 illustrates two possibilities.

Notice the basic similarity between Flow chart 2 and part of Flow chart 1. It represents a useful pattern of

Flow chart 2

Sycamore fruits are brought to school

MAKING COLLECTIONS

Can anyone find say ten sycamore fruits each different in some way? Shall we make a collection of other fruits with wings? What other tree fruits can we collect?

EXPLORING AND INVESTIGATING THE FRUITS

Which words best describe its movement through the air? Who can find the heaviest/lightest fruit? How could we weigh them? Will a heavy/large fruit fall faster than a light/small one? Will the movement alter if we remove part of the wing? Will a wet fruit fall faster than a dry one? What happens to the movement when there is a strong wind blowing from one side?

working that holds good for a wide range of situations where children contact trees.

Aim to lead initial interest in a particular thing into more detailed interest and at the same time try to spread interest to other similar things. In this way you will have plenty of possibilities for development.

Visit places where many trees grow

Is there a wood, forestry plantation or town park within striking distance of the school? A preliminary visit will reveal its potential for developing activities described in this Unit, and there may be a local expert who can help.

Useful contacts might be made with the Forestry Commission, a local natural history society, or a branch of the Aboricultural Association. Check also whether there are Nature Trails in your area; their printed guides may be of value.

Any visit to places where trees grow will yield a wide range of material for follow-up work and it is likely that trees will account for only part of the children's interest. This is an important point to note because although the Unit is restricted to activities with trees it is not intended that trees should be necessarily studied in isolation. We are concerned about the development of children's scientific understanding and from the Project's point of view, the things children achieve through working with materials are more significant than the particular material they choose to explore.

Flow chart 3 shows how work with trees was but part of the follow-up work that developed after a class of eight- to nine-year-olds visited a town park.

Flow chart 3

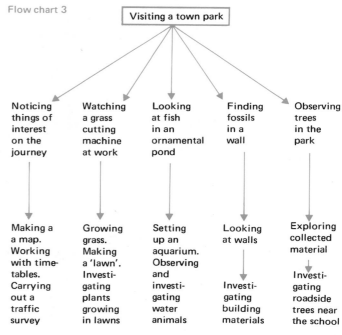

Grow some trees

Here is a good starting point for urban schools. If there are few trees in the neighbourhood, why not plant some? It's not a difficult task. Grown in pots, trees will cheer up an asphalt play yard, and planted in strategic positions they give relief to the flat expanse of grass surrounding many schools. It's wise to check first with your local authority but a parks department or the Forestry Commission may help you with planting problems. On a smaller scale, consider introducing Bonsai trees in the classroom, and remember also that many tree seeds will germinate quite readily in classroom conditions. You will find ideas for developing these activities in Chapter 4.

Lead in from other areas of work

Flow chart 4 indicates some possibilities:

Flow chart 4

NUMBER WORK	CREATIVE WORK
Using tree material for:	Using tree shapes colours, textures and material for:
Estimations and measurement Shapes, symmetry, tessellations Set and graph work Mapping	Drawing, painting, printing Embroidery, collage, claywork Creative writing, poems Making music

Exploring trees

TOPIC WORK	
For example: Our village/town:	Mapping the local environment including trees. Recording place names
People in other lands:	Finding out about life in jungles, in lumber forests, in places where no trees grow
Bible stories:	Finding out about biblical trees

Many other topics relate to trees though the links are rather tenuous ones depending on the fact that so many of the things utilised by man are derived from them. Such topics include buildings, transport, the food we eat, and common materials such as wood, paper, rubber

It may be that when working in other subject areas a real reason for observing and investigating living trees emerges. There are many possibilities but forced development from other classroom work can create artificial and spurious interest which may not prove very productive.

In this chapter we have recorded a number of starting points that could be developed in various ways. Just how things develop depends on the individual teacher but there are some aspects of organisation, implicit in the method of working, that are common to all classrooms. We shall consider them in Chapter 3.

3 Organising the work

It is easy enough to find starting points for tree work but not so easy to get a class organised and busy exploring. We will consider some ways of helping things run smoothly.

Classroom organisation

Making material provision

The children will need space to work and various materials for collecting, investigating and recording. They will also need time to do these things adequately and scope for storing work in hand. These considerations apply whatever children explore, and teachers experienced in the ways of working advocated in the Unit will have their own methods of dealing with them. For others, new to work of this kind, we recommend a look at the helpful suggestions for classroom management given in the Nuffield Junior Science *Teachers' Guide.** In addition, a preliminary survey of Chapter 7 of this Unit will help with the materials and equipment your children may require.

Getting work under way

Successful work requires talking time, and if science work is a new venture it is a good idea to begin on a small scale. Get the main body of the class working on something familiar and then try out some of the Unit's suggestions with a group. Perhaps, for example, you normally collect autumn leaves for creative work and for writing and reading about autumn things. Why not get a few children working on some of the activities of Chapter 4? If they are unfamiliar with this kind of work spontaneous comments and questions may be slow in

*Teachers' Guide 1, *Chapter 5, Nuffield Junior Science, Collins.*

coming and they will need a fair amount of direction. Talk about things they might explore and suggestions for ways of going about their tasks. Try to leave them with some definite problem that emerges from discussion. This is best expressed as a question. It might be a very simple one, 'How many of the leaves are damaged?' Or, leading from the same observation, it could be more sophisticated, 'Is there any connection between the kind of damage and the kind of leaf?'

With a definite task established the group can then work independently until they need more discussion when their activity is complete. This is the time to talk about possible records and to draw out ideas for further investigation.

It is all rather subtle and difficult to write about. To quote one teacher:

'When I started this work a few years ago I found it very hard to cope with different groups exploring different things. I never seemed to be available when I was wanted. But now it somehow happens and I'm amazed at the ideas that come from the children.'

Things do 'somehow happen' because we gradually build up experience of how children respond to particular materials, and we become more adept at guiding their lines of inquiry. But in the early stages many teachers find it helpful to prepare for likely developments by making a flow chart of things children might do and by noting some leading questions that could stimulate the activities.

The photograph shows a preparatory chart made by a teacher planning to introduce investigational work to her class of nine- to ten-year-olds. If you are hesitant about 'science' you might find it helpful to make a similar plan based on your own children's interests.

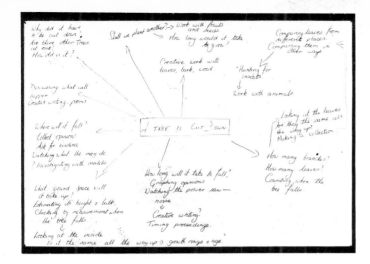

You will find many suggestions for activities and questions in subsequent chapters of the Unit.

Working with objectives in mind

What goes on in a particular classroom and how it happens depends on local circumstances, but one point of organisation is common to all classrooms. It is a concern for *why* things happen, or, put in other words, a concern for what children gain from their work.

Let us consider now what children might achieve through working with trees and how these ideas relate to classroom practicalities. The illustration below records some activities involving trees that occurred in one class during the autumn term.

Making collections of leaves and fruits

Sorting the collections

Using the materials for creative work

Reading and writing about autumn things

The activities are typical of many classrooms, and if we were to ask 'what might children gain from them?,' different teachers would have different replies, for achievement can be expressed in many ways. But from the Project's point of view it is most usefully considered in terms of the *objectives** implicit in children's work. Applying this idea to the activities shown in the illustration on page 7 we might produce a list which contains the following objectives.

Some objectives implicit in the activities shown in the illustration on page 7

Willingness to collect material for observation or investigation.

Interest in comparing and classifying living or non-living things.

Ability to record impressions by making models, painting or drawing.

Awareness of seasonal changes in living things.

Ability to use books for supplementing ideas or information.

Willingness to assume responsibility for the proper care of living things.

Ability to classify living things and non-living materials in different ways.

Ability to use histograms and other simple graphical forms for communicating data.

Awareness of sequences of change in natural phenomena.

Ability to select relevant information from books or other reference material.

Now the objectives we have listed may appear to be pedantic statements for interpreting classroom activity, but in practice they form a helpful framework for thinking about children's achievement.

Notice that although the children were working with trees there is no mention of trees in the list. This is significant.

If we interpret children's activities with a particular material in terms of the underlying objectives we can better appreciate how specific work contributes to their general development of scientific understanding.

Notice also that the objectives of the list are arranged in two sets. Again this is significant. It relates to the idea that since children vary in ability they will show varying stages of achievement in their science work. And in this context the Project has chosen three stages* for considering children's development of scientific understanding. The stages relate to their mental development and are not tied to chronological age.

So the list of objectives on the left reflects the certainty that for any one class there will be children at different stages of scientific understanding. The first five objectives are relevant to children at Stage 1: the others apply to Stage 2. But it is by no means certain that the listed objectives were achieved through the activities illustrated. They are merely objectives implicit in the situation and we should need to know more of what went on in the classroom before we could assess their possible achievement. Nevertheless, the example illustrates an important point:

Thinking about objectives in relation to classroom activities can help us ensure that children's science work is appropriate to their stage of mental development.

We shall consider some practical applications of these points.

*The objectives are taken from the Project's guide to Objectives for children learning science which is reproduced at the back of this Unit.

*For further detail see With objectives in mind and the guide to Objectives for children learning science.

Using objectives as a 'check-list'

Here is a flow chart recording the activities of the illustration on page 7.

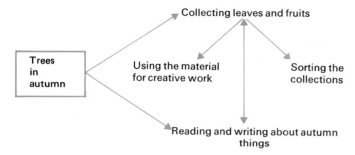

If you relate what the children did to the objectives at the back of the Unit, you will find more objectives implicit in the work than those we listed on page 8.

At the same time you might also notice some objectives not apparently covered by the activities though they could be applied to situations where children work with tree materials in autumn. The *ability to find answers to simple problems by investigation* is a good example. There are no activities recorded which are likely to promote the objective and so, in a sense, the children have missed out on certain experience. This is an important observation because it can set in motion a useful train of thought:

'If it is a worthwhile objective could the children get experience relevant to it when they next encounter tree materials?'

'. . . maybe their spring work with sticky buds and other twigs could develop into problem solving situations . . . ?'

'Have they had any relevant experience in their earlier work? Could they gain it in subsequent topics? Perhaps if we develop a project on buildings I could get some investigational work going with building materials . . . ?'

'Next time I do trees in autumn maybe I could think out some investigations . . .'

The example serves to illustrate how an appraisal of possible objectives can pinpoint opportunities for learning that might otherwise be missed.

But we are not implying that every piece of work should provide opportunities for achieving every possible objective. Clearly this is impracticable. What we are suggesting is that the Project's objectives can be used to check whether or not children are getting an over-all 'balanced diet' of science experience.

Why not use objectives as a check-list for your children's science work?

Using objectives when planning work

Let us consider the case of a teacher planning work based on a group of trees growing near her school.

Some ideas for work readily present themselves without recourse to objectives. The children could for example compare the tree barks, describing them and taking rubbings. These are activities long established by practice.

But there are other possible activities which might well be overlooked because they relate to fairly abstract ideas. And it is here that objectives can be useful. Let's take one as an example:

Ability to predict the effect of certain changes through observation of similar changes.

If we are aware of this as a worthwhile objective in the development of children's scientific understanding then we can look for opportunities to develop work in which children consciously predict change. Perhaps they could make paintings predicting what their trees will look like in say three months' time? . . . perhaps from their observations of seedlings growing near the trees they could make predictions in changes that will occur in acorns they plant themselves? . . . perhaps? . . . In ways such as this we can use objectives to think out activities which are not on first thoughts obvious ones.

Now objectives have another useful function when we plan work; they can help us cater for the progressive use of the same material.

Consider for example a teacher introducing winter twigs into her classroom. Usually she will plan her work so that children have opportunity to observe and compare them and to talk about the changes they notice as the twigs develop. If we think about these activities in terms of objectives we will find that they relate to Stage 1. But there may be children in the class who are ready to progress further. Can we cater for them using the same material? A scrutiny of Stage 2 objectives may suggest possibilities. For example:

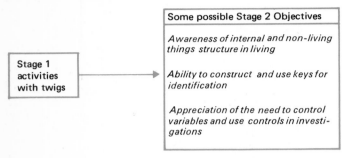

Stage 1 activities with twigs →	Some possible Stage 2 Objectives
	Awareness of internal and non-living things structure in living
	Ability to construct and use keys for identification
	Appreciation of the need to control variables and use controls in investigations

With particular objectives in mind we can turn our thoughts to practical activities that might help their achievement. The chart on the right indicates some possibilities.

Teachers new to science work may find these ideas complex, but familiarity with the contents of the Unit should make things clearer. We have developed the example in some detail because we wanted to illustrate how thinking about objectives can help us cater for progression in the use of materials.

Understanding the role of objectives in the Unit

In this chapter we have set out some ways in which working with objectives in mind can enrich classroom activities. We hope that teachers will find the ideas useful ones to apply in their own classrooms. But it is important to get the Project's objectives in their right perspective.* They are not statements to be slavishly worked towards. Neither are they infallible landmarks in a rigid scheme for describing children's scientific

For further detail see With objectives in mind.

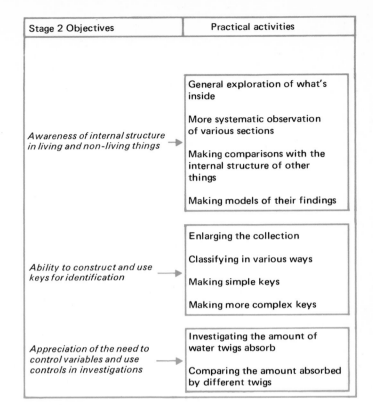

Stage 2 Objectives	Practical activities
Awareness of internal structure in living and non-living things	General exploration of what's inside More systematic observation of various sections Making comparisons with the internal structure of other things Making models of their findings
Ability to construct and use keys for identification	Enlarging the collection Classifying in various ways Making simple keys Making more complex keys
Appreciation of the need to control variables and use controls in investigations	Investigating the amount of water twigs absorb Comparing the amount absorbed by different twigs

development. Quite simply they are guidelines for thinking about the kind of science that is appropriate for young children.

In subsequent chapters we shall concentrate on things children might *do* when working with trees, but it is worth recording that they have been developed by applying objectives in ways described in this chapter. So although you will not find many specific references to objectives in what follows, you can be sure that they underlie all the practical activities we suggest.

11

4 Autumn activities

Working with leaves

Looking at falling leaves
If it is possible let children stand under a tree and really look closely at leaves as they fall.

Making general observations
What words best describe the movement of a falling leaf?

Can anyone catch one?

Can anyone hear a leaf fall?

Do more leaves fall from one part of the tree than from others?

Do more land in one place than in other places?

How many fall in say two minutes? This is seemingly a simple problem, but let the children suggest ways of solving it. They will have to devise some co-operative method of working which enables all the leaves to be counted and which ensures that no leaf is counted more than once. It is also worth discussing whether one record is a fair representation of the amount of leaf fall.

Encourage work that involves comparing observations of one tree with those of other trees.

Which local tree do they think will be first to lose all its leaves? Which will be last?

Which trees are likely to keep their leaves throughout the winter? Someone might make a plan to record the predictions for checking at a later date.

From such general observations more sustained investigations could develop and it is a good idea to keep in mind the objectives which relate to devising experiments. They will help you guide activities. Here are some suggestions.

Investigating how fast leaves fall
For example:

Do big leaves fall faster than small leaves?

Do leaves of one shape fall faster than leaves of other shapes?

Let the children devise their own methods of working. Initially they will probably just take a couple of markedly different leaves and drop them to the floor to see which lands first. Discuss with them whether or not their test is a fair one. Is the distance they used sufficient to make any differences obvious? Can they rely on one result? And what exactly were they investigating? Perhaps it was big and small leaves . . . so what do they mean by 'big'? Is it the area of the leaf that is important? Is it the weight that matters? Could they make their work more quantitative?

They might try investigating whether or not variation in leaf area or weight affects the time taken for leaves to fall.

They will need to take measurements.

Area is easy: they need only make a leaf outline on squared paper and count the squares. But see what they suggest.

13

Weighing a single leaf will present more problems. Encourage suggestions. They might end up with a technique of the kind shown below.

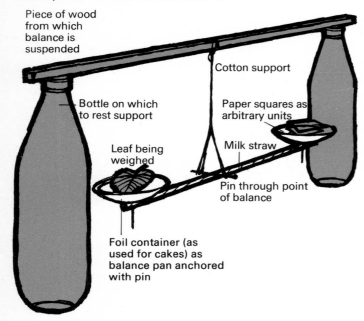

Piece of wood from which balance is suspended

Bottle on which to rest support

Cotton support

Paper squares as arbitrary units

Leaf being weighed

Milk straw

Pin through point of balance

Foil container (as used for cakes) as balance pan anchored with pin

With some quantitative method established they are all set for further investigation.

This sequence of suggestions illustrates a progression from Stage 1 to Stage 2 activities. The extent to which children can cope with variables* in an investigation is an indication of their stage of development. And their response in a situation where they discuss variables in their work and how far they have controlled them is in a sense a diagnostic opportunity for a teacher. Children who are unable to suggest ways of making their investigation 'fairer' or who apparently see no point in doing so are at an early stage in their understanding of science—though it could be that they are bored with the material. In any event, it's an opportunity to note their response, to provide additional Stage 1 experience and to keep Stage 2 objectives in mind for them at a later date.

*For further details see Working with wood Stages 1 and 2, page 10.

Finding out how many leaves fall
Do more leaves fall on certain days than on others?

The central problem here is an obvious one; they cannot stand under a tree all day counting leaves. How then might they estimate its daily leaf fall?

Encourage suggestions. Here are some made by top juniors:

'You could count all those that fall in half an hour and then multiply to get how many fall in a day.'

'You could clear all the leaves from under the tree after school and then see how many are there after school tomorrow.'

'You can't count out all the leaves. We could clear a bit of ground and count the leaves that land there. Then we could work out how many fall all around the tree.'

Work of this kind is valuable experience of estimating and sampling. Have discussions about what seems to be the best practical method to use and talk also about its limitations. Try to arrive at some working technique that gives a rough assessment which can be used for further investigations.

Is it true that most leaves fall on a windy day?

Do more fall on wet days than on dry days?

Is it perhaps a combination of things that affects the number of leaves that fall from a tree?

What things might be important?

Is there any connection between the numbers that fall and the strength of the wind? . . . the direction of the wind?

They will need things to assess wind speed and direction. If they have had earlier experience with anemometers and vanes they will know what to use; if they are new to these measurers they will enjoy constructing them.

Two simple constructions are shown on the next page.

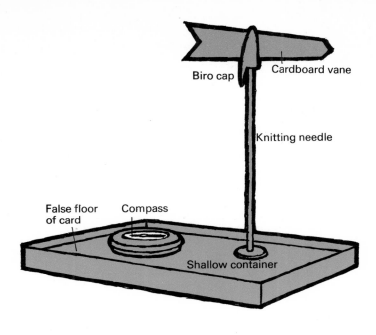

Biro cap
Cardboard vane
Knitting needle
False floor of card
Compass
Shallow container

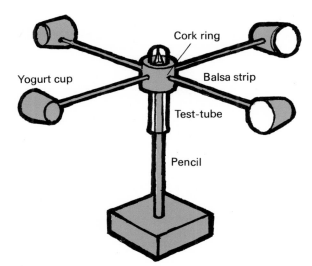

Cork ring
Yogurt cup
Balsa strip
Test-tube
Pencil

The value of the children's work comes from the total learning that goes on when *they* attempt to solve problems. To do this they will need time to try out ideas and time to make mistakes. And this is a point that bothers many teachers. Is the time well spent? Certainly, if we were only concerned with factual answers to questions children investigate then there would be

much time wasted. But if we have a variety of objectives in mind for them, then time expenditure is an important and necessary feature of their work.

Thinking about why leaves fall

Collect opinions from the children for they may promote investigations, but remember that the full explanation of why leaves fall is a complex one and, like the answers to many 'why' questions, it is beyond the understanding of young children.

'I think it's because they get dry like plants at home if you forget to water them.' Louise.

'It's when they've finished changing colour. They just drop off.' Alan.

Such comments invite exploration.

Are freshly fallen leaves drier than leaves still on the tree? Could the children devise ways of assessing 'dryness' in leaves? Here's scope for ingenuity.

Is it true that only leaves that change colour fall from trees? Here is a need for further observation.

Try introducing some leafy twigs into the classroom if they can be obtained without damage to trees.

When will the leaves fall?

Do they fall before leaves still on the tree? If there is a difference what might account for it? Is it because the classroom is warmer? . . . drier? . . . or might it be because the classroom twigs were damaged when they were taken from the tree? Here's a situation full of variables and if the problem generates sustained interest it offers opportunity for further development.

Encourage critical discussion of any results the children obtain. Remember that their findings will be 'right' for the methods they use, though they may not get the correct answer in terms of more sophisticated knowledge. Try to develop in them an attitude of the kind 'when we did . . ., we discovered. . . . it *might* mean . . . .' In this way we can help them appreciate the inadequacies of making generalisations from limited evidence.

Discovering what happens to fallen leaves

Have discussions about man's use of fallen leaves. Talk about bonfires and compost heaps.

Why not make a bonfire? How easy is it to burn fallen leaves? The activity will teach children a lot about the properties of materials. Encourage 'before and after' observations. How much space does the unlit bonfire take up . . . how much is left after burning?

Has anyone a compost heap at home? Does it contain any of last year's leaves? Consider making a compost heap at school. Everyone could bring in some leaves and a group could make the heap in some little-used place in the school grounds. It's best to pile the leaves in some container that allows air to circulate. A slatted wooden fruit case is very suitable. Someone might like to glean information about compost heaps from gardening books. They may encounter reference to the compost 'activators' that are sold in gardening shops.

Does an activator really speed up decay? Perhaps someone could design an experiment to find out. *Note.* Do check, from the label, that any activator you get is safe to handle.

Try to include as many different kinds of leaves as possible in the compost and keep one of each sort for future reference.

Once made the compost heap will have little appeal until things start to happen, but have a good look at it in the spring.

Have some leaves decayed more readily than others?

Has anyone noticed how warm the compost feels?

Why not use the home-made leaf mould for growing bulbs and other plants?

Do not forget the animals in the compost. You will find many suggestions for working with them in the Unit *Minibeasts.*

If there are trees conveniently near your school encourage observations of leaves that have fallen.

Try 'adopting' particular leaves and keep a check on what happens to them over a period of time. Children

will have to devise ways for locating their own leaf.
Here are two possibilities: there are others.

Paint spot
(also on
under surface)

or

Name tag

Simon

Do some leaves decay faster than others? Encourage
suggestions for activities that might answer the
question.

In one school a group of children put different kinds of
leaves in a nylon mesh bag to keep them from blowing
away and pegged the bag into the ground under a tree.
They chose to make observations every week and
discovered that their beech leaves were last to decay.
Other children might have other suggestions. And they
might get different results.

Exploring leaf litter
Choose a sunny day and a time best suited to the local
trees. If they still have an accumulation of the previous
year's shed leaves it is best to explore them soon after
the first leaf fall. If, as in a town park, the trees have
none of the previous year's leaves underneath then it is
best to wait until most of the current year's leaves
are shed.

Looking at the leaves
How many different *kinds* of leaves can the children
collect from under one tree? Where has each kind come
from? Encourage a search for parent trees.

Which is the commonest leaf present? Try visual
estimations and see how they compare with counting
and sampling techniques.

One class of top juniors decided to record all the leaves
within a circle of roughly 6 m. They ran out 6-m lines

17

from the trunk and enclosed the area with string. Next they made a plan for dividing the area into sectors and subdivided each section. They counted all the leaves present.

Surprisingly the children found more willow leaves under their oak tree than any other kind of leaf and so set off on further explorations.

Another class of juniors tackled the same problem in another way. They decided that it was impossible to count every leaf, but that they could count all the leaves in a small area and use their findings to work out the total number under each tree. They were then faced with the problem of deciding where to make their count and much discussion took place.

Some wanted to count an area where there was an obviously high number of different leaves, others with some feeling for systematic working said this was not fair and perhaps they should take several counts and then average their results. At this point their teacher steered their discussion into a consideration of random sampling and the children decided to make ten counts for each tree in random places. But a new problem then emerged. How best to establish randomness? There were several suggestions and finally they decided to map the area under the tree and divide it into small numbered sections. They wrote the numbers on separate bits of paper and put them in a hat. Finally they held a draw and the first ten numbers drawn from the hat were used to locate places where they would do their count. Other children might work out other ways of achieving random counts.

Searching for animals
Most of the animals in leaf litter are very small and children will have to look really closely to find them.

Try giving them some challenge. Can anyone find an animal that hops?... that wriggles?... that does not move at all?

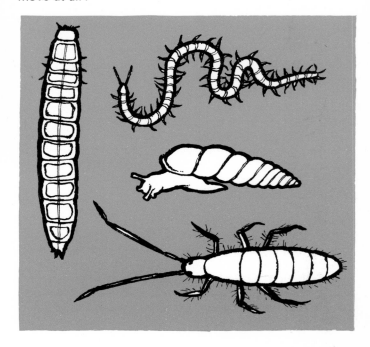

Encourage on the spot observations and take some leaf litter back to school for the children to examine at leisure. They will find things best if they search through small amounts of litter spread out on a light-coloured background. But be careful not to let the material get too dry or the animals will be killed.

Some children would enjoy setting up an 'animal extractor' of the kind shown below. Any animals in the litter move away from the heat and light and collect in the container.

Leaf litter

25 W bulb

Tall container to prevent catch escaping

You will find many suggestions for working with the animals in the Unit *Minibeasts.*

Making and using leaf collections
Children spontaneously collect autumn leaves that 'look pretty', 'feel nice' or are in some way 'interesting' and these collections have great potential for follow-up work. But it is also profitable to channel their interest into making specific collections which encourage detailed observation and give greater awareness of the variety of living things.

Here are some possibilities:

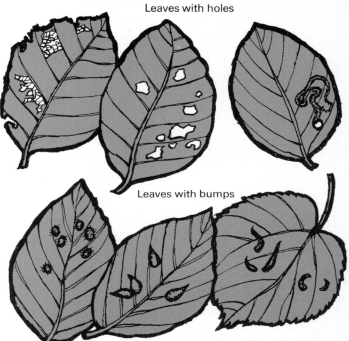

Leaves with holes

Leaves with bumps

Try also challenges of the following kind:

Who can find: the biggest leaf? ... the smallest leaf? the leaf that has most colours? ... that has the fewest colours? the leaf that ...?

Can anyone find two leaves that are *exactly* alike?

Encourage discussions about the leaves children collect. Usually their immediate interest will focus on features which lend themselves to creative work, and they will enjoy making prints on paper, fabric and in clay.

Teachers will class these follow-up activities as art and craft work. And so it is, but it also provides valuable incidental experience of the properties of things which is part of developing scientific awareness. So look for opportunities to extend this general awareness of properties and encourage activities which make children consciously consider particular features of leaves in ways that increase their observational skill and their ability to classify information.

Consider chances to *order* observations. Here's one of many possible examples:

Which is the shortest, say beech, leaf in the collection? Which is the longest? How do other beech leaves compare? Try making a long line of leaves arranged in order of length. It will look impressive and could lead to further activity for able children.

What's the most common length of a beech leaf? Children could perhaps sort the collection into length classes and count the number of leaves in each class.

If they graph their findings for say 100 leaves the results should give a normal distribution graph, which is valuable experience of variation.

Encourage also *sorting* activities. Let children experiment with their own groupings but look for opportunity to extend their observations. The illustration at the top of the next page shows some possibilities.

Try to avoid sorting based on pedantic niceties. Technical terms such as pinnate, palmate, simple, compound are best left to a later stage when they are

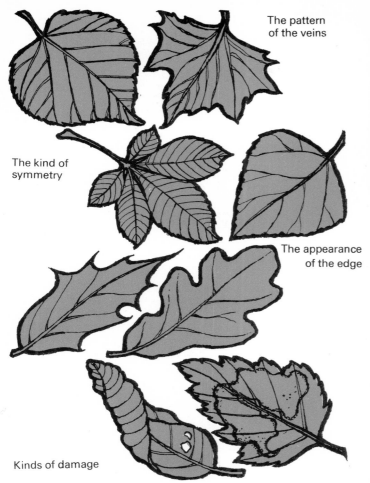

The pattern of the veins

The kind of symmetry

The appearance of the edge

Kinds of damage

When thinking about leaves as thin structures it is a natural progression to consider just how thin they are. Children might devise some method for measuring the thinness or thickness of a leaf. Here is one possibility:

needed for more detailed work. Concentrate on things that can be observed, remembering that observation can include noticing what happens when things are done to the leaf. Try, for example, sorting on the basis of what happens when water falls on different leaves. Try other things.

Sorting activities tend to emphasise differences between leaves but biologically the most significant feature is not that they are so varied but that basically they are thin and flat. It is a good idea to introduce activities which help children appreciate this fact. Try including other materials in leaf-sorting activities so that a set is obtained in which all things are thin and flat.

If they measure the thickness of a certain number of leaves they can divide the measurement by that number to get an approximation of the thickness of one leaf.

Many children will find the task difficult. But the value of the work lies in recognising a problem and attempting to solve it. The actual thickness of a leaf is in this context of minor consequence and so little is gained by giving them ready-made apparatus which does the job for them. And here, as with so many of the Unit's suggestions, we are back to its underlying theme: it all depends on the objectives we have in mind.

Working with fruits

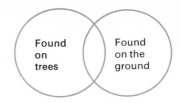

Many of the activities we considered in the previous section apply equally to work with fruits. But fruits unlike leaves do not all obligingly shed themselves from trees at roughly the same time in the school year, and so some of the suggestions in this section could be developed at other times. We shall consider fruits as a source of autumn activities because children are sure to come across them in their explorations of leaf litter, and because interesting examples are most readily available at this time of year.

Collecting fruits
A hunt for fruits has little appeal if it is introduced 'from cold', so try to develop collections from events that stimulate particular interest. A conker craze is a good example. Remember also that a collection of *observations* can sometimes be as productive as actual material.

Collecting information about local fruit
Just how many different kinds of tree fruits can the children discover locally? Encourage activities that involve them in classifying their observations. They might make lists.

Equally they could record their observations by sets and look for overlaps.

It is a good idea at the same time to make a note of local trees without fruits. Be sure to date all records for they will be useful for later comparisons.

When considering local sources of fruits do not forget the greengrocers.

Which of the fruits for sale grow on trees?

Which of them are home-grown? Which come from abroad?

Foreign fruit will make a good supplementary topic that encourages reading for information and the use of maps.

Where do the fruits come from? A collection of labels will help.

What do the fruit trees look like?

Perhaps someone in the class has recently arrived from overseas and could contribute some first-hand details.

Similar studies could grow from a survey of tinned fruit at home or from the canned fruit in a supermarket.

Making special collections
Many of the activities of pages 19–20 are relevant here. Aim to build up increasing awareness of the fallen fruits children discover, supplementing their collections where necessary to provide wide variety. Look also for opportunities to develop problem-solving situations.

Try collecting different examples of one kind of fruit to give children experience of the wide individual variation that exists. Conkers are particularly productive whilst sycamore and holly berries make interesting examples for discerning eyes.

Encourage comparative observations of size, shape and colour patterns and be ready to lead children's comments into investigational work.

'Last year I had a twelver.' John talking about conkers.

What is it that makes a high-scoring conker? Is it its size? . . . its age? Is it true that baking them or soaking them in vinegar improves their performance? Could the children devise a 'fair' test to find out? They will have to sort out the variables involved and devise some way of eliminating human interference in their test.

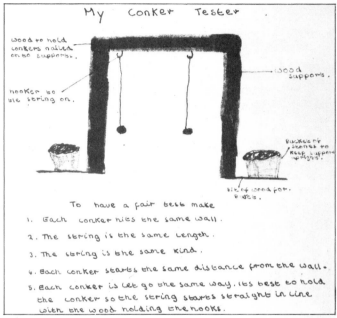

My Conker Tester

wood to hold conkers nailed on to supports.

wood supports.

hooker to tie string on.

buckets of stones to keep supports upright.

bit of wood for rests.

To have a fair test make

1. Each conker hits the same wall.
2. The string is the same length.
3. The string is the same kind.
4. Each conker starts the same distance from the wall.
5. Each conker is let go the same way. Its best to hold the conker so the string starts straight in line with the wood holding the hooks.

'They're bright red so the birds can see them.' Ann commenting on holly berries. Do birds eat the berries? Here is a chance for further observation. Can birds see colour? Here is opportunity for investigation. What would be a fair test?

Make a collection of edible fruits. Consider fruits eaten by man and those eaten by other animals. Be sure to include nuts, and look for examples which give clues to who's been eating them.

Oval hole with serrated edges of long-tailed field mouse

Large irregular damage of squirrel

Tiny hole of nut weevil

Let the children look closely at the teeth marks. Perhaps they would like to observe their own. A good bite on

soft chocolate will reveal the pattern of their front teeth and some volunteer might make an impression of his complete set by biting on *new clean* Plasticine or freshly made pastry. The impressions can then be filled with plaster of Paris to make a cast. The result will delight the children and undoubtedly lead to an enthusiastic interest in teeth.

Whilst on the subject of fruit eating why not see if birds fancy any of the fruits children collect. Try putting various kinds on a bird table or on ground visible from the classroom. Do any disappear? Could any of these have been taken by birds? What happens if they use the *seeds* from the fruits?

Consider special collections based on the movements of fruits. Which can be blown through the air? . . . rolled down a slope? . . .

Sycamore wings are particularly interesting. Try exploring the way they fall. What happens if one of the wings is removed? What happens if the fruit is waterlogged?

Children will likely bring in cones to add to fruit collections, and this raises an interesting point. Technically, cones are not true fruits because, although they contain seeds, their seeds are not completely enclosed as they are in 'real' fruits. But this is a pedantic distinction for young children; sufficient for teachers to be aware of it and to use their judgement about its implication for classroom activities. Certainly it is worthwhile encouraging conscious awareness of the difference but it is not something to overplay at an early stage. Concentrate on features with more immediate appeal.

Make a cone collection.

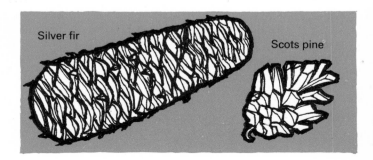

Silver fir

Scots pine

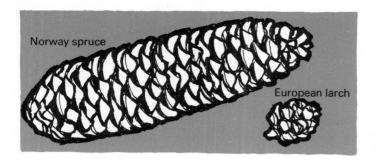

Norway spruce

European larch

Let the children sort the collection in various ways, they will have lots of ideas. Encourage them to look closely at the way cones open. Do they first open at the top? . . . the bottom? . . . all over? Do all cones open in the same way?

Is it true that the opening and closing of cones can be used to forecast weather changes? Put some cones outside and see what happens over a period of time. Will similar cones kept in the classroom behave the same way? Just how reliable are cones as weather fore-casters? The children will have to keep sustained records to find out. They will gain valuable experience of thinking critically about their work and of interpreting trends in collected data.

Finding out about tree seeds
Making general explorations
What is inside tree fruits? Let the children find answers by squashing, crushing, cutting or any other method they think suitable. They will soon discover that the insides of different fruits are quite varied. Talk about the things children notice and be ready to extend their observations.

They will notice that seeds vary in size. How small are the smallest? How do they compare with others? Here is opportunity for lots of estimation and measuring.

They will also make comments about the numbers they find. Which fruit has most seeds? Which has fewest? Do all fruits of the same kind have the same number of seeds? Try collecting seeds from apples and oranges.

When interest is focused on seeds consider activities that help children appreciate how trees fit into a pattern

of plant relationships. Talk about other plants with seeds and plants that have no seeds.

Why not make a collection of seedless plants and see how many fruits children can collect from plants other than trees? The collections will stimulate all kinds of work.

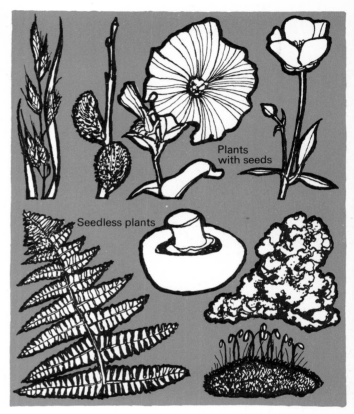

Plants with seeds

Seedless plants

Look also for opportunity to consider the link between flowers and fruits. Children will be familiar with this sequence of events in familiar plants but can they relate it to trees? Who has seen the flowers that made the seeds they have discovered? Many will link conkers with chestnut tree 'candles' but few will have noticed less conspicuous tree flowers.

Make a record of 'unknowns' and see what can be found out about them. Encourage the use of books and first-hand observations in the spring.

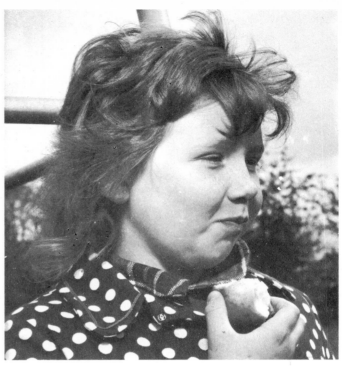

The tuck-shop provides material for investigating seed variation

Planting seeds

My Oak Tree

The oak is born and I watch it day by day
At first it is young and tender
But as the days pass and turn to weeks
And then to months and then to years
I see it mature and its roots are firm and its wood
thick

I see it grow and wait for the day when I can proudly
say it was I who planted it
Say that I helped it to grow into a tree big and fine
Say that when the rain did not come it was I who watered
it

And when people look at it and say it is a fine tree
I will hold my head up high

Try planting a wide range of different seeds just to see what happens. Some will germinate and some will not, and this makes a good talking point. But ensure success with some by including examples that germinate readily the first spring after the fruits have formed. Oak, sycamore, beech and horse-chestnut are very suitable. Elm and ash will also give results if they are planted when the fruit is green; older fruits will not germinate for a further eighteen months. Try also apple and orange pips and perhaps an avocado.

Aim to provide a variety of material for comparative observations, and activities which help children appreciate conditions necessary for germination and the time factor involved. Look particularly for opportunities to develop experimental situations.

Have discussions about what the seeds should be planted in. Encourage children to bring in suitable containers for this will establish a personal involvement in the enterprise which is very necessary to sustain their interest in the period when 'nothing happens'. King-sized yogurt pots with a drainage hole cut in the bottom make cheap and adequate containers. Get ideas from the children about the kind of soil they should use. Perhaps parents who are keen gardeners can enlarge their suggestions and maybe provide some seed compost. Include, if possible, soil from where the fruits were found and while collecting it why not plant a few seeds there for later comparisons?

As planting gets underway have a discussion of how the seeds should be planted. Be sure to have some sown about 5 mm deep in a natural position, that is the position they normally take up when they fall from the

trees. But encourage investigations also. Does it matter if the seeds are planted upside down? What happens if they are put in at different depths? Try sowing isolated seeds and entire fruits to see what happens. It is also a good idea to have a few planted against the sides of jam jars so that children can later observe root development.

When the seeds are planted collect opinions about the best place to keep them. Some might be kept in the classroom and some outdoors to see which develop first. And help the children make plans for looking after them. They will have to keep the plants moist but not waterlogged. It is a bit of a chore, but valuable experience in helping them appreciate the need to give living things proper care and attention. If they let them dry out there will be nothing to show for their work and nothing to see in the spring.

Getting to know local trees

Trees growing near the school have great potential for children's learning. But often they are so commonplace they escape notice. So try to develop situations in which children see the trees in a new light and want to find out more about them. Interesting work with leaves and fruits might stimulate inquiry into the trees that produce them, or some particular challenge could stimulate greater awareness.

Who passes most trees on their way to school?

Once interest is aroused there is lots to do.

Finding out where the trees grow
Making surveys
Much depends on local circumstances and an important part of the work will be discussing with children their scale of operation and the kinds of records they need to make.

Try counting trees. Select some convenient area and collect opinions about the numbers present. Let the children find out how their opinions compare with facts. In some places they can count every tree and in others they must find ways of estimating numbers.

How Many Trees In Our road?

Granny said 100.

Mummy said 45.

Daddy said 45.

John said 200.

Georgina did not know.

I said 50.

When I counted there were 78 trees, So Granny was nearest But I was next.

Progress from simple counting to surveys that classify information. Make some records that show distinctive tree features, taking suggestions from the children.

Here are some made by eight-year-olds:

'Let's mark the good climbers and the no-good ones.'   Mark.

'Pretty ones and ordinary ones.'   Emily.

'We could do it like on maps.'   Nigel.

All suggestions are worth following up. They help children systematise isolated observations.

Why not make a map of the locality which incorporates their ideas?

What symbols can they invent to show the tree features they find interesting?

How do their symbols compare with standard Ordnance Survey ones?

Have a look at a local large-scale Ordnance Survey map.

Does it show trees? Does it show how many are present?

Consider some work involving tree names, concentrating on a few trees that are easily recognisable. Make some records of where they grow and help children appreciate that tabulated observations can often give ideas for further work.

Town trees found in			
Name	**Streets**	**Gardens**	**Parks**
Plane	√	—	√
Wellingtonia	—	—	√
. . .			
. . .			

Country trees found in			
Name	**Gardens**	**Woods**	**Hedges**
Elm	—	√	√
Cherry	√		—
. . .			
. . .			

Have discussions about their findings. Are there differences in the same kind of tree when it grows in different places?

What is the commonest tree in the whole of their area? Is it the same for different places within the area? Again, tabulated records can lead to further activity. Here's a record made by some country children.

Place	Commonest tree
Maskells Wood	Pine
Park Wood	Oak
Park Farm Hedge	Elm
Drove Road Hedge	No trees

They were disappointed that Drove Road hedge had no trees and wrote to the farmer to ask why. He told them it was a young hedge kept in shape by a mechanical trimmer. His information opened up other lines of inquiry including a special survey of hedgerow trees and some sophisticated work in which the children approximated the age of a hedge by its trees.

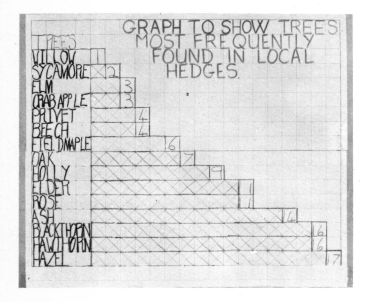

GRAPH TO SHOW TREES MOST FREQUENTLY FOUND IN LOCAL HEDGES.

TREES
WILLOW
SYCAMORE 2
ELM 3
CRAB APPLE 3
PRIVET 4
BEECH 4
FIELD MAPLE 6
OAK 7
HOLLY 9
ELDER 11
ROSE
ASH 14
BLACKTHORN 16
HAWTHORN 16
HAZEL 17

Finding out about trees in past times

When children are familiar with their present-day trees why not steer them into the past? Help them appreciate the changing pattern of trees in their environment. What changes can they themselves recall? Do they know of any trees that have been cut or blown down? Are they aware of any new plantings? Were there fewer or more trees in the locality when, say, their grandparents were at school. Let them talk with elderly residents and see what information they can collect.

Try comparing the trees of old streets and those of new estates. Are there differences? They will likely discover that recently planted street trees tend to be smaller to accommodate modern traffic.

Go further back in time by consulting old maps and getting clues from street names. The local museums or parish council may have useful source material. Can the children find evidence of change?

Which is the oldest tree in the locality? What events has it lived through? Encourage a search for information about very old trees.

When did the very first trees occur? Can anyone find out details of fossil trees? Are there likely to be any in the neighbourhood? The time-scale of such events is a difficult concept for young children, but their work will help them appreciate patterns of change.

Left: Major oak, Sherwood Forest. This tree has been linked with the legend of Robin Hood

Opposite: The three photographs show the disappearance of wooded areas in one locality

30

Late 19th century map of Norwood, South London

Present day tree-less street in Norwood

Recent aerial view of part of the locality covered by the map

Adopting trees

Encourage children to 'adopt' a few local trees and get to know them really well. Start in autumn and then there is a whole year to make occasional observations.

Noticing special features

Have a look at tree shapes. How are they best described? Are they strong . . . . flexible shapes?

Count the main branches and notice how they grow from the trunk. Do they grow upwards, downwards or straight out?

Let children record their observations through artwork. Try making paper sculpture trees. Try also capturing the 'feel' of trees by paintings that involve only say ten brush marks.

Talk about the parts underground. How far out do children think the roots travel? Perhaps someone could hunt for pictures of tree roots.

Let the children examine bark to see what they can discover. Encourage comparative observations. Is the bark the same all over? How does the bark of one tree differ from that of other trees? Make rubbings and look for chances to collect bark from fallen branches, but do not let children peel bark from living trees. Help them appreciate the damage this causes and encourage a search for damaged trees in the neighbourhood. Why not build up a dossier of tree vandalism?

Try using bark for dyeing. Which bark gives the best dye?

Have a hunt for animals. There will not be many about in autumn, but this is worthwhile experience for later comparisons. If the children find some it is a good idea to make some records of how many they saw and whereabouts they occurred.

Do not forget the plants growing on and around the tree. They have little immediate appeal for children at this time of year, but some incidental observations will be valuable for comparisons at a later date. Concentrate on the different *kinds* children notice, for they will not be able to identify them all.

How many different kinds grow on the tree?

How many grow underneath?

Which is the commonest plant?

Finally, see what children can find out about the tree's wood. Is it used for anything?

It is a good time of year to consider man's use of trees for much of the work is indoor activity best undertaken when bad weather prevents outdoor exploration.

You will find suggestions for activities relating to the timber man uses in the Unit *Working with wood Stages 1 and 2*, but remember also the aesthetic value of trees.

Have discussions about tree motifs decorating everyday things. Encourage a search for examples in fabrics, wallpapers, crockery. Perhaps children could make their own designs based on the features of their adopted trees?

Making measurements
How tall are the trees? Start with children's opinions and rough approximations made by comparing their height with that of the trees they want to measure. Perhaps someone can find out how Boy Scouts find the height of trees? Lead on to a quest for greater accuracy. Some might use a ruler as a simple sighting device.

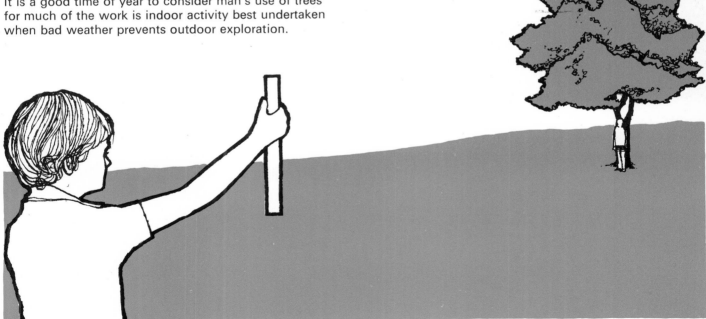

Here is the procedure:

1. Someone acts as marker and stands under the tree.

2. His partner, the measurer, moves to where he can see the marker and the top of the tree.

3. The measurer holds the ruler vertically at arm's length and sights its tip on his partner's head and puts his thumb on the ruler where the marker's feet are sighted. This gives him a sighting length for the marker's height.

4. The measurer then sights up the tree counting how many times he uses the sighting length to reach the top. This number multiplied by the marker's height will give the approximate height of the tree.

Using a hypsometer

Older more able children will enjoy making special equipment for measuring heights. They might make clinometers or construct a hypsometer.*

How fat are trees? Let children encircle the tree with outstretched arms; if they measure their arm spans they can work out its approximate girth.

They will get greater accuracy by measuring its diameter with tapes and callipers.* Try not to let tree measurement become measuring just for measuring's sake. Look for opportunity to involve children in devising their own techniques. If, for example, they have used

*Details for construction and use are given in Chapter 7.

sighting estimations for recording heights, perhaps they could invent some sighting technique for estimating the diameter of trees quickly.

One group of children made sighting cards by marking a 'tree trunk' on a wall and finding out the width of card that just obscured the tree trunk when it was held out at a particular distance from the 'tree'. They then prepared a set of diameter-cards to use at different distances.

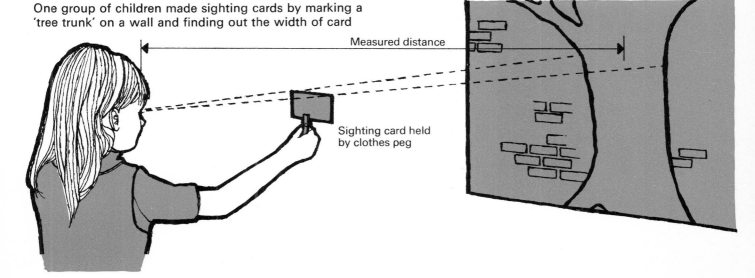

Measured distance

Sighting card held by clothes peg

Another group constructed a sighting screen for use at a particular distance, on which they marked reference lines from which to make direct estimations of the diameter of their trees.

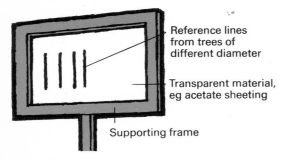

Reference lines from trees of different diameter

Transparent material, eg acetate sheeting

Supporting frame

How far does the tree spread? Here is another problem that can be treated at varying degrees of sophistication, depending on the children's experience.

At a simple level the whole class could stand round the tree, positioning themselves under the tip of the outermost branches. Let them consider the area they enclose and decide how best to estimate it.

More systematic work could entail setting out to plot the area. In this case the children will need to start with some reference lines and work out what measurements they must take in order to make a plan.

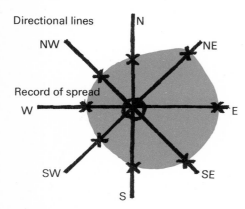

Directional lines

N
NW
NE
Record of spread
W
E
SW
SE
S

The finished plans may show clearly that the tree spreads more in one place than another, and here is a start for further investigation. Perhaps it is because some parts get more light than others? Perhaps it is something to do with some parts being more sheltered than others? Perhaps all trees of the same kind grow like that in any case? Able children might pursue these ideas.

How much wood is there in a tree?

Let children suggest ways of calculating how much wood is present. Someone might discover how foresters and timber merchants work it out. At the same time they might find out information about the cost of various timber and apply it to their trees.

'My tree is worth £200.'

'Mine's not worth anything but it's nicer than yours.'

Planting trees

Home-grown trees

This section is based on the work of one top junior class in a city school. They had no neighbouring trees to adopt so they decided to grow some. The flow chart below shows what took place and provides a useful guide to teachers planning similar work.

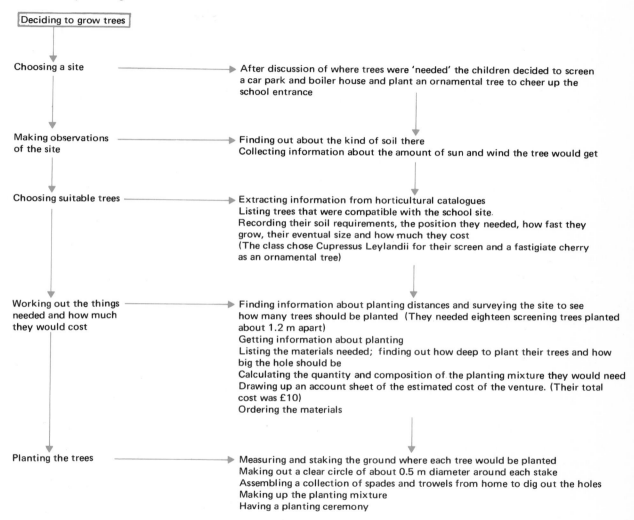

Deciding to grow trees

Choosing a site → After discussion of where trees were 'needed' the children decided to screen a car park and boiler house and plant an ornamental tree to cheer up the school entrance

Making observations of the site → Finding out about the kind of soil there
Collecting information about the amount of sun and wind the tree would get

Choosing suitable trees → Extracting information from horticultural catalogues
Listing trees that were compatible with the school site.
Recording their soil requirements, the position they needed, how fast they grow, their eventual size and how much they cost
(The class chose Cupressus Leylandii for their screen and a fastigiate cherry as an ornamental tree)

Working out the things needed and how much they would cost → Finding information about planting distances and surveying the site to see how many trees should be planted (They needed eighteen screening trees planted about 1.2 m apart)
Getting information about planting
Listing the materials needed; finding out how deep to plant their trees and how big the hole should be
Calculating the quantity and composition of the planting mixture they would need
Drawing up an account sheet of the estimated cost of the venture. (Their total cost was £10)
Ordering the materials

Planting the trees → Measuring and staking the ground where each tree would be planted
Making out a clear circle of about 0.5 m diameter around each stake
Assembling a collection of spades and trowels from home to dig out the holes
Making up the planting mixture
Having a planting ceremony

The children became very enthusiastic about their 'own' trees and trees in general and went on to grow Bonsai trees in the classroom.

Not all teachers will be able to operate on such a scale, but do consider planting even one tree. It is not a difficult task because the case-history provides a general model for operations and local horticulturalists can help with details. Even urban schools with no soil available could try their hand at tree growing in pots. Children delight in the venture and the newly planted trees will provide useful material for later investigations.

5 Spring activities

Working with twigs

Make a collection of different twigs being sure to cut them cleanly from trees to prevent damage. It is best to collect them with unopened buds when there are a few buds open on the trees so that things soon happen in the classroom.

Keep the twigs in water in see-through containers and give them an occasional rinse to remove dust.

Exploring their structure

Encourage comparative observations and look for opportunity to steer general comments into more detailed awareness of the material. But be careful not to stultify interest by undue emphasis on technical terms. Aim to get children working in a spirit of inquiry.

Examining buds

Which twig has the biggest buds? . . . which the smallest? Talk about their shapes and what they feel like.

See who can identify various twigs when they are not allowed to look, but only touch. General experience of this kind builds up an awareness of variation in living things and can become a springboard for more detailed study.

How many buds on the twigs?

Do twigs of the same length always have the same number of buds?

How far apart are the buds?

Which twigs have buds growing close together? Which do not? Here is a place for simple sorting which could be the start of key-making activities described on page 45.

Let children look really closely at one large bud to see what they can discover. Horse-chestnut buds are best to use because of their size; their stickiness can be removed for easier handling by soaking the buds overnight in methylated spirits. Talk about the number of parts the children notice and the way they are arranged.

Perhaps someone would like to find out what is inside? The task requires a fair amount of manipulative skill and it is useful to have some tweezers available to help things along.

They will proceed in a haphazard manner but when they discover differences in the inside parts, some may want to begin again and work more systematically. If this happens they will enjoy making a permanent record of their work. The bits can be stuck in order on card with Copydex and covered with a plastic seal. It will be a useful record for discovering what happens to the various parts when they see other buds opening.

A few children find this detailed work fascinating; they might explore different buds in a similar manner.

Finding scars

If children handle sticky bud twigs someone is almost sure to comment on the marks under the bud and this can start off more activity.

Let them hunt for marks on all their twigs. They will find some under buds and some in rings around the twig. Perhaps someone could find out from books what they are called, for here is a case where acquiring information can lead to extended observations.

Able children might collect evidence that leaf scars under buds really have been caused by leaves dropping off. They will need to keep watch on things that happen later when the twigs grow.

Others might explore the ring scars which are sometimes called growth rings. Can they work out, through observations of developing buds, what has caused the scars? Encourage close observation with a hand-lens. The keen-eyed may find a pattern in the arrangement of marks in the growth rings. Is it the same for all twigs?

Include in their collection of twigs some with two sets of growth rings. How far apart are they? The distance represents one year's growth and discussion of how much trees grow can lead to further exploration.

Do all twigs from the same tree grow the same amount in one year?

If there is a tree nearby in an exposed place it will probably reveal very marked differences between twigs growing in different positions.

Do twigs from one kind of tree make more growth than twigs from different kinds?

Problems such as these are sophisticated ones for young children and are quite meaningless if they are introduced before the children have wide general experience with twigs. If, however, as a result of earlier experience they become interested in a quest for detail the problems are within their capabilities and have value in helping children appreciate how isolated observations fit into wider patterns.

Noticing changes
Investigating developments

Keep a watch for opening buds, encouraging comparative observations and an awareness of the sequence of changes that occur.

The five photographs below show the development of a horse-chestnut bud

Which kind opens first? . . . which next? . . . which is last?

Do buds growing outside open in the same order?

Try to develop inquiry situations, however simple.

Do big buds open before little ones?

Is there any connection between the position of a bud and how soon it opens?

Is the old weather saying true?

'If the oak's before the ash
We are going to have a splash.
Ash before oak
We will have a soak'.

When the buds open let the children observe how the leaves unfold.

Which kind of bud has most leaves?

Are all the leaves in a bud the same?

Do they all grow in the same manner?

Can anyone find ways of recording how much they grow?

Make some outdoor observations.

Do all the buds on a tree open at the same time? If not can the children find a pattern in differences they notice?

Can they suggest reasons for it that could be investigated further?

Encourage observations of newly developing shoots.

Keep records of how the new leaves change as they get older.

Hunt for new shoots on evergreen trees and compare the new and old leaves.

Keep a look out for tree flowers. Many children are surprised that 'ordinary' trees have flowers. They may be familiar with fruit tree blossom, conspicuous catkins and chestnut 'candles', but others pass unseen.

Increase children's awareness of tree flowers by a search for local examples. If they have adopted trees make some dated records of when the first flowers appear and notice whether or not the trees have leaves and flowers at the same time.

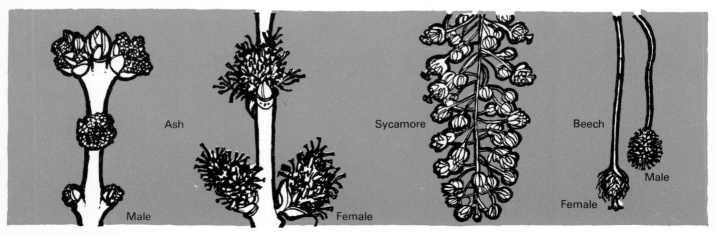

Ash   Male   Female

Sycamore

Beech   Male   Female

Are the flowers easy to see?

Let children examine tree flowers with a hand-lens. How many different kinds of parts are there in each flower? Perhaps some nimble-fingered person would like to tease the flowers apart with needles.

The findings make a useful permanent record if the various parts are stuck on card with Sellotape.

Encourage a search for information about tree flowers.

List common trees with just one kind of flower and look for local examples.

Can anyone find out the names of trees which have two different kinds of flowers growing on them? . . . the names of trees that have two different flowers, but each grows on a separate tree?

Have discussions about what will happen to the flowers and if possible give children opportunity to watch developments as flowers change to fruits.

Through work of this kind children build up experience of the variety of living things and their sequential patterns of development.

Finding out about twigs and water
Twigs kept in classrooms inevitably need watering and here is a natural starting point for investigations.

Where has the water gone? Collect opinions and put some to the test.

'The twigs drink it.'

'It goes into the air.'

Does the water disappear into the air? . . . the twig? . . . both?

Have discussions of ways of finding out and let children explore their own ideas, looking for opportunity to develop the notion of a 'fair test'. If they work fairly they will have to sort out the variables in their problem.

Does water disappear if there's only water in the container?

Does it disappear if there's a twig present but escape to the air is prevented? Children may not know how to achieve this; a layer of oil will do.

How can they be sure that any water disappearance is due to the things they investigate? They'll need to set up some control container with no twig in water and the water surface protected with oil.

The drawing below shows the experiment arranged by a group of top junior children, but it must be strongly emphasised that the value of the work lies not in children carrying out 'set-pieces' but in the thought and discussion that goes into planning it.

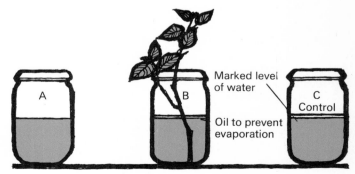

Children will get evidence that twigs absorb water and it is a natural development to think about where the water goes. Can they suggest ways for exploring its journey?

'You could make a hole further up and see if the water comes out.'

Comments such as this show how little children appreciate the internal structure of things. But others may have experience they can transfer to the problem.

'You could colour the water and see where it goes.'

This comment was made by a girl who had seen dyes used for tracing underground streams.

Try colouring the water with water-colour paints, food dyes, ink and anything else the children suggest, and if possible, include some eosin which is sure to give results. It is best to use leafy twigs for the 'pull' of water is greatest when the leaves are actively transpiring.

Leave the twigs in the coloured water for a day or so and then cut them up to see what has happened. Children usually expect to see a uniform colour inside and are surprised that this is not so. Discuss their results, for they can lead to further work. Look at the twigs that have changed colour inside and notice where the colour is.

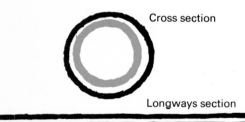

Cross section

Longways section

Talk about any twigs without colour. Perhaps the colouring they used could not get through. Here is opportunity to investigate the properties of the various colourings they used.

If the children are enthusiastic about their experimental work, consider extending it. Does the colour go up all twigs in the same way or are some faster than others? Let children discuss a fair test.

Here is what happened in one top junior class. The children used beech, elm, ash and yew twigs. (It is a good idea to include an evergreen twig such as yew for it will show marked differences.) They put their twigs in eosin solution, noting the time, and after four hours they cut up the twigs to see how far the colour had reached. They worked systematically sectioning the twigs 1 cm at a time and recording whether or not there was colour present.

Colour level	Beech	Elm	Yew	Ash
1 cm	✓	✓	✓	✓
2 cm	✓	✓	✓	✓
3 cm	✓	✓		✓
4 cm				
etc.				

They then made a block graph to show how far the colour had travelled in each twig and found that beech was the 'fastest', ash next, then elm and yew was last of all.

Other children might get different results. Help them to realise that because their evidence is limited, they cannot draw general conclusions from it.

Would they get the same result if they repeated the experiment?

Would they get different results if they used fatter twigs? . . . longer twigs? . . . twigs with more leaves?

Perhaps someone would like to find out?

Work of this kind gives children useful experience of experimental procedures and increases their awareness of the organised internal structure of things.

KEY I

Branches with needle-like or scale-like leaves

1 {
Leaves needle-like .... see **2**

Leaves scale-like .... see **19**

2 {
Needles long (1–6 in.), **in closely set bundles with 2 or 5 in each bundle**.................. ...(Pines) see **3**

Needles shorter (½–1½ in.), some in clusters on dwarf shoots, and others singly on long shoots .(Larches) see **9**

Needles in whorls of 3, awl-shaped .... **Juniper** (pages 34–35)

Needles single .... see **10**

3 {
2 needles in each bundle .... see **4**

5 needles in each bundle .... see **8**

4 {
Cones and side branches only at the tip of each year's long shoot .... see **6**

Cones and side branches also in the middle of the more vigorous long shoots .... see **5**

Example of an identification key taken from *Trees and Bushes* by Vedel and Lange, published by Methuen

A biological key is simply information arranged in such a way that it can be used to identify unknown specimens.

Most keys work by asking pairs of questions about the specimen and according to the answer the reader gives, they direct him by number to other questions until eventually he reaches the correct identification. For brevity the questions are usually implied ones written in the form of statements.

Now keys may seem complicated things to include in a book concerned with young children. Certainly most published varieties are beyond their understanding, because they use complex language and demand very detailed observation. But the *principle* of key construction has great relevance because keys are based on the systematic arrangement of information and any child who has experience of sorting and recording is quite capable of making a key, however simple it may be.

The value of the work lies in the experience of classifying and organising data; it will also help children's later use of complex keys by giving them familiarity with basic principles. So consider introducing some key-making activities, but be sure they arise from

things children are involved in, or else the work is little more than an academic exercise.

Activities of the kind described on page 39 could provide a starting point, or children might be stimulated to make keys through seeing their teacher use one. Many are intrigued that an apparent 'mumbo-jumbo' of words and figures can provide the name of something unknown, and their interest is aroused.

Any tree material could be used for making keys, but spring twigs are possibly the best starters because they are easy to handle and are quite distinct. Whatever the children use, make sure they begin with a limited number of things that have obvious observable differences. We shall take six common twigs to illustrate key making.

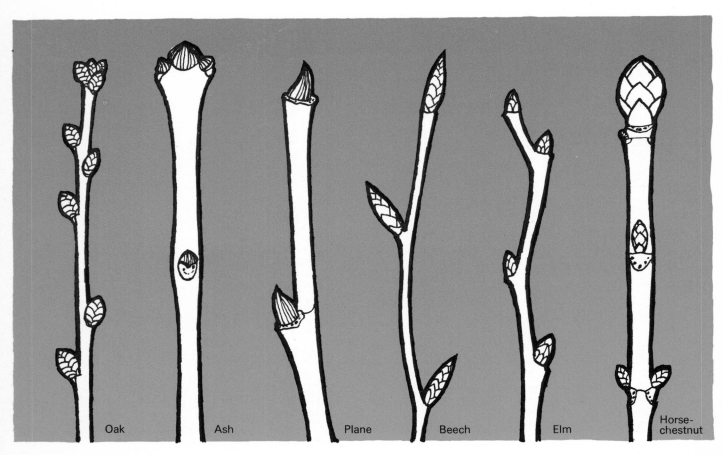

Oak   Ash   Plane   Beech   Elm   Horse-chestnut

Making keys by removing one twig at a time

Getting information

Let children examine their collection of twigs and remove one twig they consider to be very obviously different from the others. They should make a note of why they decided it was different.

Next they remove another twig, then a third and so on until they are left with six separate twigs, each of which they recognise by some special feature.

The chart on the right shows the pattern of the work and the features chosen by one group of children.

Children will take time to arrive at such a scheme; they will need lots of discussion and trial and error working. But once they are satisfied they have a satisfactory plan for separating out their twigs they are ready for the next stage.

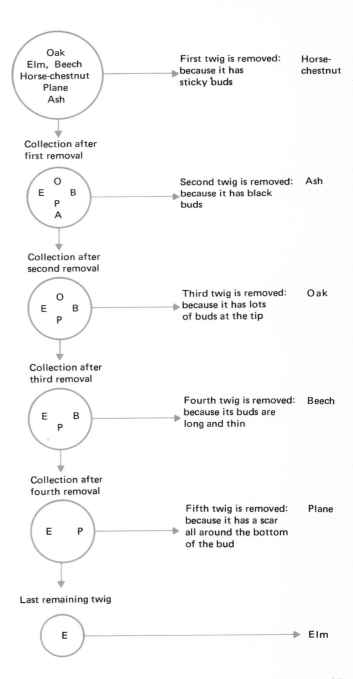

The original collection

Oak
Elm, Beech
Horse-chestnut
Plane
Ash

First twig is removed: because it has sticky buds — Horse-chestnut

Collection after first removal

O E B P A

Second twig is removed: because it has black buds — Ash

Collection after second removal

O E B P

Third twig is removed: because it has lots of buds at the tip — Oak

Collection after third removal

E B P

Fourth twig is removed: because its buds are long and thin — Beech

Collection after fourth removal

E B P

Fifth twig is removed: because it has a scar all around the bottom of the bud — Plane

E P

Last remaining twig

E

Elm

Organising the information

Help the children recall what they did to separate out each twig and get them to write out some directions that makes the reader do the same thing.

It is best to give them a format for their work to help them record things systematically. Try something along the following lines:

Which was the first twig you removed? *Horse-chestnut.*

Why did you remove it? *Because it had sticky buds.*

What will you write to make sure someone else removed the horse-chestnut twig first? *Feel the buds to see if they are sticky.*

Which twigs are left? *O   A   E   B   P.*

Now help them put their answers into a key-like construction. For example:

First   *feel the buds.*
    Are they sticky?
        Yes . . . It is horse-chestnut
        No   . . . It might be   O A E B P

They now have a pattern they can repeat for the other twigs and so produce a simple key.

First   *feel the buds.*
    Are they sticky?
        Yes . . . It is horse-chestnut
        No   . . . It might be   O A E B P

Next   *look at the colour of the buds.*
    Are they black?
        Yes . . . It is ash
        No   . . . It might be   O E B P

Next   *look at the buds at the tip of the twig.*
    Are there more than three in a group?
        Yes . . . It is oak
        No   . . . It might be   E B P

and so on.

Let other children try out the key. Does it work? Some may now be ready to extend their work, substituting number guides for the boxed information. For example:

1. *Feel the buds.*
    Are they sticky?
        Yes . . . It is horse-chestnut
        No   . . . Go to: 2

2. *Look at the colour of the buds.*
    Are they black?
        Yes . . . It is ash
        No   . . . Go to: 3

3. etc.

There are two advantages to this approach:

a. The children *gradually* build up the idea of a key. This is important for real understanding.

b. The statements in the key are introduced so that decisions can be made in answer to questions on directed observation. This helps to establish them as statements requiring decision.

Children who have made this kind of key might now be ready to use a simple printed key* but probably they will first need experience of making keys by systematically excluding groups of specimens.

Making keys by removing groups of things

Children will find these keys more difficult because they involve a more complex handling of information. Instead of removing one twig at a time they need to divide their twigs into two groups and then systematically divide each subgroup. Let them explore ways of doing this and so get information for making a key. The chart on the next page, top left, shows how some able top juniors made their groupings. Other children might have other ideas.

For example: Winter Key to Some Common Deciduous Trees, *School Natural Science Society Leaflet No. 22.*

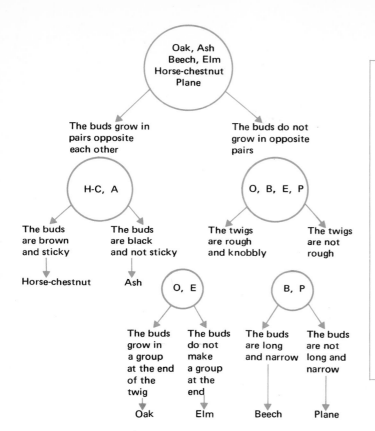

Oak, Ash
Beech, Elm
Horse-chestnut
Plane

The buds grow in pairs opposite each other

The buds do not grow in opposite pairs

H-C, A

O, B, E, P

The buds are brown and sticky

The buds are black and not sticky

The twigs are rough and knobbly

The twigs are not rough

Horse-chestnut

Ash

O, E

B, P

The buds grow in a group at the end of the twig

The buds do not make a group at the end

The buds are long and narrow

The buds are not long and narrow

Oak

Elm

Beech

Plane

When they have worked out a way of subdividing their collection they are ready to organise their ideas into a key-like form. Build on their earlier experience and help them decide what statements they will use to guide the reader. For example, the first grouping in the chart could be recorded as:

Buds grow in opposite pairs on the twig.

Buds do not grow in opposite pairs.

Initially they will have problems in numbering their key but if, through earlier work, they understand the guiding function of numbers they will soon see the need to 'number out' systematically successive information about the groups. They will find things easiest if they first 'number out' the subgroup with the fewest subsequent divisions, which in our example is horse-chestnut and ash.

Here is how the procedure works:

1. Buds grow in opposite pairs on the twig . . .   2
   Buds do not grow in opposite pairs . . .   (3)
   This statement is not numbered until the twigs relating to 2 are keyed down further.

2. Buds brown and sticky . . .   Horse-chestnut
   Buds black and not sticky . . .   Ash
   Now they have accounted for all the twigs relating to 2 and can use the next available number, in this case 3, to number the unnumbered statements about twigs that do not have opposite buds. They can then go from there.

3. Twigs rough and knobbly . . .   4
   Twigs not rough and knobbly . . .   (5)
   Left unnumbered until 4 is keyed out.

4. Buds in a group at the end of the twig . . .   Oak
   Buds not in a group at the end . . .   Elm

5. etc.

Now they can confidently approach printed keys to identify *unknown* twigs, though they may need help with some of the technical terms used. This gives a tremendous sense of achievement.

Making punched-card keys
These keys are arranged for the quick retrieval of information.

Preparing the cards
Let the children examine their twigs and record things they notice.

About ten different observations will do, but make sure they include some distinctive statement about each twig.

Next they must list their statements on cards, arranging them so that each can be followed by a punched hole near the edge of the card.

They will need one card for each twig, and should be

Black buds	0
Brown buds	
Buds in pairs	0
Buds not growing in pairs	

A completed card for ash is shown below:

Black buds	0
Brown buds	
Buds in pairs	0
Buds not growing in pairs	
Twigs knobbly	
Twigs smooth	0
Buds in groups at the end of the twig	
Buds not in groups at the end	0
Buds long and narrow	
Buds not long and narrow	0

careful to arrange the statements so that the punched holes on all cards coincide. At this stage they will have six identical cards.

Black buds	0
Brown buds	0
Buds in pairs	0
Buds not growing in pairs	0
Twigs knobbly	0
Twigs smooth	0
Buds in groups at the end of the twig	0
Buds not in groups at the end	0
Buds long and narrow	0
Buds not long and narrow	0

Now they must prepare a separate card for each twig. To do this they read each statement in turn to see if it is correct for the particular twig. If it is they leave the punched hole intact; if it is incorrect they extend the hole to the edge of the card.

Using the key

The cards are piled on top of each other with the holes carefully aligned and a knitting needle is used to extract information. Suppose a beech twig is being tracked down using the list of statements on the card. The first statement *black buds* is not appropriate and is ignored. The second *brown buds* is appropriate and the needle is pushed into the hole right through the pile of cards.

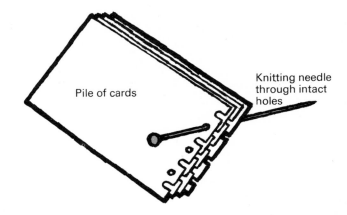

Pile of cards

Knitting needle through intact holes

The pile of cards is then shaken. Those with complete holes remain on the needle; the rest fall off.

The procedure is repeated for other statements until only one card is left—beech.

If the children enjoy their key-making, perhaps someone would like to construct keys for tree leaves, or tree fruits? Remember the value lies in their making and it is not a process that can be rushed.

Getting out and about

Observing trees in bad weather

Looking at frost and snow
Encourage observations of frost and snow patterns. Which trees display the most patterns? Let children suggest possible reasons for things they observe and help them put their ideas to the test.

Try comparing the effect of a heavy snow fall on different trees. Which tree holds most snow? How much does it hold? Some children might devise ways of estimating the weight of the snow; others its volume, but all will have practical problems to overcome.

If they find marked differences let them try to account for them. Is there any connection between the amount of snow on a tree and its shape? . . . its position? . . . whether or not it has leaves? . . . other things?

Consider a hunt for animal tracks around trees. It is not very feasible as a whole class activity but some children might carry out explorations in their own time and report back. Ask them to collect information about the shape of the tracks, how deep they were, and how far apart.

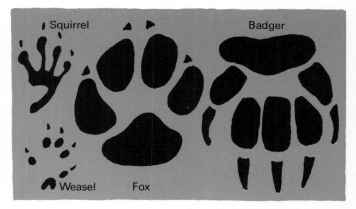

Children enjoy investigating their own snow tracks. How do they alter when they walk slowly, walk quickly and when they run? It is fun activity that encourages careful observation and it may throw new light on the tracks of other animals. What kind of movement do they represent? Were the animals moving quickly?

Watch for when the snow melts. Whereabouts on the tree does it first start? Collect opinions about which local tree will be first to lose all its snow and which will be last. Are the children guessing or are they making predictions based on evidence? There is scope here for lots of valuable discussion and further exploration.

Watching rain

Have discussions about trees on rainy days. Which are good to shelter under, which are not? Talk about what happens to rain falling on a tree. Does it reach the ground? Let children discuss ways of investigating the problem. They will need some means of measuring rain that falls on open ground and methods for estimating how much rain gets through the tree.

In one class someone suggested putting a bucket under a tree and another in the open to see how much each collected. Everyone thought this a good idea and their teacher let them go ahead although she knew it was not a very accurate method. When the children got outside they argued about where to put the bucket under the tree, for they quickly noticed that it would collect more water in certain places than in others. This made them amend their original idea and they ended up sampling the water running down the trunk and dripping from the branches in order to estimate the total amount involved.

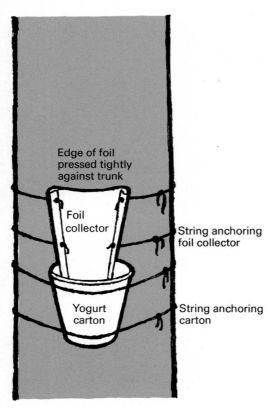

Edge of foil pressed tightly against trunk

Foil collector

String anchoring foil collector

Yogurt carton

String anchoring carton

Their work illustrates children operating at an early stage of scientific understanding. Through doing things they saw limitations to their plan that were obvious to an adult but which they were unable to grasp before going into action. As a result they improved their method of investigation. It's a good example of 'learning by doing'.

When children observe rain running down a tree trunk, let them notice the patterns it makes. Does any get in through the bark? Could they devise a fair test to find out? Encourage suggestions.

Here is how two boys went about the task. They used logs for their investigation deciding that if they put a log in water and any got through the bark the log would get heavier. They were careful to make the test a fair one by varnishing the cut ends to stop water getting in that way. As they were getting the log ready for its experiment, one boy suggested that it might be a good idea to see what happened if they also used a similar log with its bark stripped off, so they could be sure that any change was due to the bark.

Log with bark intact

Water

Sealed surface

Log with half bark removed

Weight

They weighed the logs, left them soaking for a week and then reweighed them. The work of these lads could be described as Stage 2 in nature for they showed an awareness of variables in a problem and a concern for controlling them. Other children might have other ideas for approaching the problem.

Finding out about communities

Spring is a good time for observing trees to find out how they and other plants and animals live together. There will not be too much undergrowth to impede explorations and much of the work will have additional value as a basis for interesting comparisons in summer.

Aim to build on earlier isolated observations of the plants and animals associated with trees and help children become increasingly aware of the inter-dependence of living things.

Considering animals

Keep a watch for nest-building in local trees. Rooks' nests will be the most noticeable and if you are lucky enough to have some near the school do keep a diary of events.

When does the first activity take place?

How many birds are involved?

Are they more active on certain days than on others?

How long does it take to build the nests?

How long are they occupied?

Do other birds go near the tree when the rooks are there?

Is it true that 'when the rooks build high we are going to have a good summer'?

Perhaps someone can discover what materials rooks use to make their nests. Why not put some out to see if the the birds take them? Try other things as well.

Encourage reading for information.

Which other birds build nests in trees?

How are the nests recognised?

Which birds have names that suggest they are associated with trees?

Do any occur locally?

What do they feed on?

Are any harmful to man's interest?

Look for signs of the activity of mammals.

Have a 'detective' hunt for tracks, droppings and fur.

Try to locate places where the animals live and if you are fortunate and find dreys or burrows let children observe them closely; try to lead their observations into inquiry situations.

A squirrel's drey

Let children collect information about mammals that live amongst trees. They could find out about our native woodland animals that one seldom sees, and maybe take this further in a quest for knowledge of jungle animals.

Do not forget the very small animals. They are not easy to spot so concentrate on particular places. Try hunting for those associated with bark and help children appreciate what is needed in their search by showing them how to look closely and patiently in the crevices. Their findings will make an interesting comparison with a similar hunt in summer.

Consider also a search through leaf litter (see page 18). How do things compare with what was found in autumn?

Finally, in a concern for animals associated with trees, remember the two-legged variety. Look for examples of how man's activity has affected the trees and their surroundings. Hunt for signs of tree felling, trampling and deliberate vandalism.

After children have gained some experience of various animals, encourage activity that helps them appreciate how they fit into a wider community.

Try making a woodland frieze. Everyone could choose a different animal and put it in an appropriate 'home'. The result will reinforce early ideas about the inter-dependence of living things and it is great fun to produce.

Considering plants
Start when someone notices a particular plant growing on a tree, or stimulate activity by pointing out something of interest.

Fungi, climbing plants and mosses are all worth exploring and it does not matter whether or not you know their individual names; there is lots to do without identifying them.

Jew's ear fungus

Children find fungi* particularly fascinating and the flow chart below shows ways of developing their interest. It also provides a pattern of work that can be applied to other plants.

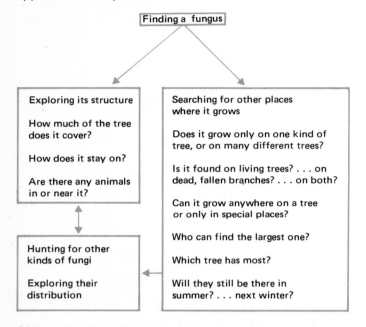

Finding a fungus

Exploring its structure

How much of the tree does it cover?

How does it stay on?

Are there any animals in or near it?

Hunting for other kinds of fungi

Exploring their distribution

Searching for other places where it grows

Does it grow only on one kind of tree, or on many different trees?

Is it found on living trees? . . . on dead, fallen branches? . . . on both?

Can it grow anywhere on a tree or only in special places?

Who can find the largest one?

Which tree has most?

Will they still be there in summer? . . . next winter?

Observational work of this kind helps children appreciate the distribution of particular plants associated with trees. They could also profitably explore some particular communities.

Make some observations of all the plants growing under one tree. Which kind is commonest? Which least common? Any work that involves children in making comparative assessments of the numbers of different kinds of plants they discover growing together will help their later understanding of ecological relationships.

Try listing say the six most common plants in order of frequency. If their names are unknown why not press an example of each to incorporate in the record.

Be sure that they can identify and avoid contact with poisonous varieties. They should treat all fungi with respect and wash their hands after handling them.

How do the findings compare with plants growing under another tree of the same kind? . . . with a different kind of tree?

Will they be the same in summer?

Encourage observations that link the seasonal appearance of trees to changes in the plants associated with them.

Keep watch for spring flowers. What is the tree like when they first appear? What is it like when they have finished flowering?

Records will help children see patterns in their observations.

Look for places where the natural growth of plants growing under trees is disturbed. Notice how plants alter near paths and consider investigating the effects of trampling.

Let children mark out a *small* area and completely destroy the plants by walking over them. Make observations over a period of time to see what happens.

Which of the original plants survive?

Do any different plants start growing there?

Have discussions about the need for responsible behaviour in the countryside.

Do not forget to look for seedlings under trees. Are there any that have come from other trees? Where are their likely parents?

Try to link children's observations with earlier ones made on fruits.

How do the numbers of seedlings compare with the numbers of fruit they saw? Consider marking some of the seedlings and keeping records of how they develop. Perhaps someone would like to work out ways for measuring how much they grow?

Encourage observations that make children more aware of the varying height of the plants around them.

How many different plants are taller than they are?

Which is tallest?

How many are shorter?

Which is shortest?

Can they arrange the commonest plants in order of height?

Observations such as these will help their later appreciation of the stratification of vegetation in ecology. Perhaps someone would like to make a scale model of their findings?

6 Summer activities

This is the shortest activity chapter in the Unit, which may seem odd since the summer term could be considered an ideal time to work with trees. But many suggestions in the previous chapters are equally relevant to summer events; we have included them earlier to encourage useful seasonal comparisons which can only be made if the activities are introduced before the summer term.

In this chapter then we will consider things which are most profitably carried out in summer, leaving teachers to decide whether or not they would like to incorporate earlier suggestions into their work at this time.

Exploring country trees

Investigating trees and light
Keep in mind the objective 'development of the concept of environment'. When used by biologists, environment is a collective term for all the conditions in which an organism lives. It includes living things, inanimate material and less tangible things such as air, temperature and light.

Children readily observe the association of other living things with trees, but the non-living factors are less obvious, though they may vaguely notice their affects. Try then to make them more consciously aware of these environmental factors of which light is probably the most significant.

Looking at shadows
Choose a hot sunny day and take children into woodland from open ground. Talk about the differences they notice and focus attention on the change in light conditions. Discuss what causes it and see which trees let a lot of light through and which do not. Let children stand under a tree and look up at the sky. (Make sure they do not look directly at the sun for this will damage their eyes.)

How much sky can they see? They cannot measure the amount but they can assess it. They could use comparative terms . . . not much, a lot, or others of their choosing. Will they see the same amount if they look up through different trees? Perhaps someone could develop a 'sky measurer' to make comparisons easier.

Have discussions about what stops the light getting through and develop inquiry situations.

Do trees that stop most light have most leaves? The children will have to work out ways of estimating the number of leaves on a tree. There are several possibilities.

Is it the number of leaves that is important or is it their size? Or is it just the total area of all the leaves on a tree? How will they work out the total area? It is a nice exercise in computation.

Encourage observations of how the leaves are arranged. Help them notice that in general they are positioned so that the upper surface gets most light. Some children might like to look more closely at the upper and lower surfaces. Can they notice any differences? This is purposeful observation that will help their later understanding of leaf function.

Make observations of changes in tree shadows. It is best to work with free-standing trees whose shadows are well defined.

Try using a tree as a shadow stick and record changes in the length and spread of its shadow throughout the day.

Keep watch also for changes in the colour of the shadows. Someone might like to collect colour statements of various tree shadows in a wood.

Comparing sun and shade plants
Collect information about the plants growing near a tree.

Which grow only in the shade?

Which grow only in the sun?

Which grow in shade and sun?

Clear-cut distinctions between sun and shade will often be difficult to decide upon, and there is opportunity here for discussing changes in the amount of light plants get at different times of the day and during the year.

How much light occurs in different places? Children could use a photographic light-meter for comparative measurements; one calibrated in light values is easiest to use.

Or they might try making their own light measurer with blue-print paper which changes colour when exposed to light. They will need to devise some way of using the paper to assess how much light is present and a method of keeping the paper in the dark until it is needed. Here is a light measurer made by some ten-year-olds.

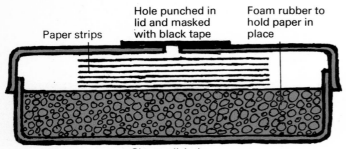

Paper strips — Hole punched in lid and masked with black tape — Foam rubber to hold paper in place

Shoe polish tin

When they were ready to use the measurer they stripped off the tape and assessed the amount of light present as the number of strips of paper that had changed colour in ten minutes. Their apparatus gave them adequate readings in normal sun and shade conditions.

Try comparing plants that grow mostly in the sun with plants of the same kind that grow in shade. Nettles, though awkward to handle, are well worth exploring and children may find other examples showing marked differences. Let them look carefully, comparing the colours, the height of the plants, and the size and texture of their leaves. If they transplant the plants will each change in the changed conditions?

Have discussions about what might have caused any differences they notice. It could be the light but it might be other things.

Help them appreciate other things in the plants' surroundings that vary, for this is good experience of environmental factors.

Perhaps one place was warmer than the other? Can they find out just how warm each is?

Perhaps one place is damper than the other?

Perhaps the soil is different in each place? Let them take some soil samples and search for differences.

Encourage general observations and also observations made by doing things. Try squeezing it, and letting water drain through it. Also consider testing the soils with a gardener's soil testing kit which will have full directions accompanying it. The children won't understand the chemistry involved, but the experience will increase their awareness of the complexity of the soil as part of the environment.

The value of this work lies in the opportunity it gives for close purposeful observation and for the chance to consider variables in a situation. But do help children appreciate that although their findings will be 'right' for the methods they used, they must not make generalisations from limited evidence.

Investigating small animal activity

Summer is the best time of year for investigating the small animals associated with trees. Make comparisons with the number and kind children found earlier and build on their explorations of where the animals occurred by investigating things they do.

Keep in mind the general aim 'posing questions and devising experiments to answer them'. You will find many suggestions for experimental work in the Unit *Minibeasts*. Here we shall merely outline a few to illustrate the approach.

Make surveys of the commonest kind of animal found in certain places. What is it about the place that the animal 'likes'? Does it 'prefer' damp or dry conditions? . . . light places or dark places? Can children devise fair tests to find out?

Collect observations of the different kinds of movement made by the animals. Does it alter when they move over different surfaces?

Which animals are active at night? Can the children devise ways of finding out? They might design some traps, but do not allow trapping just for trapping's sake, or encourage over-use of the method.

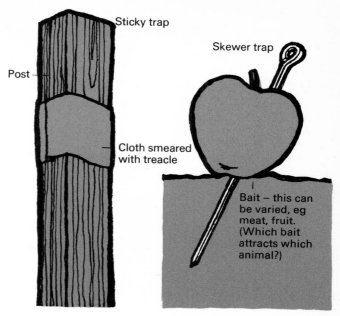

Sticky trap

Skewer trap

Post

Cloth smeared with treacle

Bait – this can be varied, eg meat, fruit. (Which bait attracts which animal?)

Be sure also to make observations of animals that become more obvious in summer. Try a search for galls; you will find the greatest variety on oak trees.

Can children discover any patterns in their distribution?

Pitfall trap

Bark to keep out rain

Jam jar sunk in soil (not too wide or catch will be eaten by larger animals)

Exploring town trees

Visiting the park

If you are lucky enough to have a large well-stocked park in the neighbourhood, some of the suggestions for exploring country trees will be possible. In addition there will likely be trees growing there that are not commonly found in the country. Get help from the park keeper and let children find out which are 'native' trees and which are trees of foreign origin planted for special effect.

Talk about their effect in cheering up the urban environment, helping children appreciate the amenity value of trees. They could try to find out when the park was opened, and who planned its landscape. Discuss with them the difficulties of deciding which trees to plant when they take so long to grow and show their mature shapes.

They might consider some local derelict area and decide how they would improve things by landscaping it with trees. They will need to find out which trees would be suitable (see page 37) and some will enjoy making a model of what their proposed landscape would look like in say fifty years' time. Work of this nature will make them aware that trees in towns do not just happen, and it may lead to a new respect of 'ordinary' trees in the street. Let them look critically at those in their surroundings. Are they well looked after?

Make a collection of the shapes of things 'planted' in pavements. Let children compare the irregular changing shape of trees with the regular static shapes of street furniture and through discussion help them appreciate the visual interest provided by trees.

The work will link nicely with activities described on page 29.

Investigating pollution

Hunt for dirty leaves. Let children explore ways of assessing how much dirt is present. They might try rubbing them with a soft white cloth to get a visual record, or perhaps wash off the dirt, collecting the dirty water in a small container. Whatever method they devise, see if they can refine it to get some standard procedure for making comparisons.

Try comparing leaves from roads with heavy traffic with those growing in minor roads.

Do some leaves collect more dirt than others?

Does more collect on the upper surface or the lower surface?

Have discussions about where the dirt comes from and make lists of local sources. If there are industrial smoking chimneys in the vicinity, keep watch for their activity. Does it affect local leaves? Is there any connection between the amount of dirt that collects and the usual direction of the wind?

Consider introducing the idea of lichens as indicators of invisible pollutants in the air. These plants are sensitive to chemicals, particularly sulphur dioxide and the kind of lichen present locally is an indication of how badly the air is polluted.

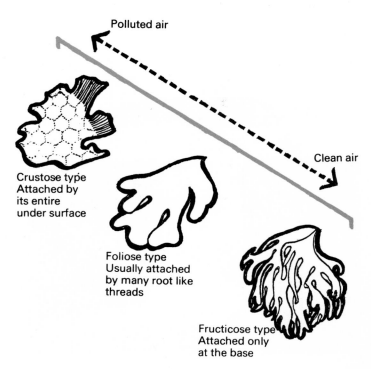

Polluted air

Clean air

Crustose type
Attached by its entire under surface

Foliose type
Usually attached by many root like threads

Fructicose type
Attached only at the base

If there is a general shortage of trees in the neighbourhood, you will probably find lichens in the churchyard, and the old stone there are also worth exploring for them. Make a survey of local lichens, recording which kinds are found and where they are found.

Are places where the lichens indicate heavy pollution also places where tree leaves are dirty?

Encourage children to look for evidence of pollution if they visit the country at weekends, and add their evidence to a larger map of the locality.

Activity of this nature will increase their awareness of the impact of man's activity on other living things.

Considering trees and traffic

Trees in towns can be traffic hazards. Have discussions about the way they affect the visibility of road users and encourage practical investigation. Exploration in the street may be dangerous, but children could simulate actual conditions by using models and toy cars.

Try to work from local situations. Perhaps there is a road junction nearby with a tree on the corner. How much does the tree affect what a car driver can see?

Let children find out road widths and the position and dimensions of the tree and make a 'mock-up.'

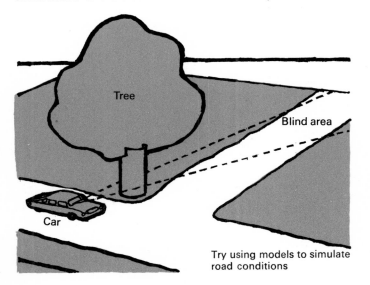

Try using models to simulate road conditions

When a car turns into the side road how much of the road is invisible to the driver?

How does the 'blind space' alter when the car goes round the corner?

Similar studies might be made from a pedestrian's viewpoint.

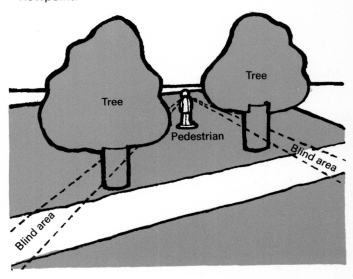

How does the 'blind space' alter when the pedestrian changes his position?

While in a road-safety frame of mind, do not forget the hazard of wet leaves on roads. Perhaps someone could simulate the situation and devise ways of investigating their effect on braking and stopping distances.

Finally be on the look-out for ways in which town trees have been pruned and lopped to decrease their hazard to traffic. Compare their shape with free-growing trees of the same kind, and have discussion about the kind of tree best suited to modern traffic conditions. It will help develop 'awareness that many factors need to be considered when choosing a material for a particular use'.

It might also generate a concern for existing trees that will be welcomed by corporations constantly bothered by vandalism caused by young people.

Making special visits

Consider organising a visit to some place where trees are grown on a commercial scale. It can be an exciting trip and through talking to experts children will learn something of the special tasks associated with large-scale tree cultivation.

They can find out about particular jobs needed for the yearly maintenance of trees and get information about the harvesting, destinations and use of the products.

Visiting a forestry plantation

The Forestry Commission has many areas of woodland where they encourage school parties, and will usually provide a guide. Why not explore local possibilities? There is such a lot to learn on the visit and children will return reeling with facts and impressions. The flow chart below shows the topics covered by one class.

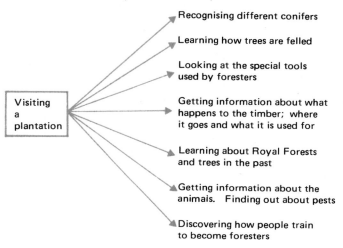

Remember also that there are Nature Trails in certain forests, for the Forestry Commission is committed to the idea of recreational woodland. Why not take the class round such a trail and let them keep their eyes open to see if people are using the area responsibly?

If the children enjoy the visit, as they are sure to, why not encourage them to set up their own trail among local trees. Other children would enjoy using it.

Visiting an orchard
An orchard is not so spectacular as a forest but it does have lots of interest. Arrange the visit just before fruit picking when there's most to see and do. It is usual for someone to show you round and children can get information about such things as:

Looking after the trees throughout the year.

Special jobs and special tools.

Growing young trees.

Methods of harvesting and packaging.

Special pests and how they are controlled.

Try to get permission for the children to explore one small area at leisure. They will likely find small animals they have not seen on their local trees, and the trees themselves can be usefully compared with those they've investigated before.

How much fruit is there on one tree?

Can they find examples of damaged fruit?

If it is possible take some things back to school to promote follow-up work. Try to get healthy fruit and damaged fruit and any special materials used for packing.

Keep any damaged fruit under upturned jam jars and let children watch what happens. It will most likely grow moulds, and here is the start of many further explorations.

Can they make a healthy fruit 'catch' the damage?

Do other kinds of fruit develop the same kind of moulds when they are damaged?

Encourage investigations of packing materials, supplementing the collection with other examples from a local greengrocer.

Are they good for protecting the fruit against damage?

Do they stop it getting damp? Which keeps out most water?

Do they stop it getting bruised? Which is strongest?

Are they easy to handle? How heavy are they?

This kind of work helps children's 'awareness that many factors need to be considered when choosing a material for a particular use'.

Use the healthy fruit to develop work relating to man's use of tree materials. It will link well with that described on page 22.

Try making a collection of say apples or plums, and explore differences between cooking and 'eating' varieties. Why not make some jam? There's a lot of number work involved and opportunity for investigation.

What happens if children vary the proportion of the ingredients?

Does the jam set? Does it stay runny?

Which jam is 'runniest'? Can they devise a fair test for comparing different jams?

Now testing runny jam may seem to be an odd, and perhaps pointless, activity for children working with trees. But if we ask 'what are they achieving from their work?' and consider it in terms of objectives, its value becomes apparent.

7 Materials and equipment

The following lists make a comprehensive guide to all the materials and equipment mentioned in the Unit.

Things for collections

Polythene bags in various sizes for plants.

Small containers with lids, for animals. Drug tubes from chemists are suitable.

Paint-brushes, spoons and pooters for removing animals without damaging them.

Plastic buckets and large strong polybags for soil and leaf litter.

A trowel, and perhaps a spade.

Notebooks and, if possible, a cheap camera for collecting observations.

Things for investigations

Readily available materials
Jam-jars and other see-through containers of standard size.

Other varied containers, including yogurt pots.

A slatted wooden fruit box.

Scissors, craft knife, tweezers.

Things for making coloured solutions.

Varnish, modeller's size tin of waterproof paint.

Plaster of Paris, Plasticine.

Measuring tapes of varying length. These deteriorate if used among damp plants, so plastic clothes-lines are useful.

Rulers, or sticks of known length for estimating heights.

More specialised materials
The following will be needed if you wish to pursue some of the more detailed investigations in the Unit.

Things obtainable from an educational supply source*
Thermometers. 'Ordinary', and a maximum and minimum.

Stop-watch.

Blue-print paper.

Eosin solution.

Things obtainable from local sources
Photographic light meter calibrated in light values. This is expensive and best borrowed from a friendly photographer.

Gardener's soil-testing kit and compost 'activator' from horticulturalists or the gardening department of a chain store.

Large-scale Ordnance Survey map of the locality from a bookseller or nearest HM Stationery Office.

For example: Philip Harris Limited, Ludgate Hill, Birmingham 3; Griffin & George Limited, Frederick Street, Birmingham B1 3HT.

Things for constructing apparatus

Simple tools.

Adhesives, nails and panel pins.

Wood offcuts and card.

All the apparatus referred to in the text is accompanied by diagrams showing how it is constructed, with the exception of the hypsometer and callipers referred to in Chapter 4.

Making and using a hypsometer
You will need:

A long tube; a chart tube is suitable.

Wood or card for making the scales.

Something to hold the scales in position; strong elastic bands will do.

Thread or wire for the sighting device.

A small heavy object for a plumb-bob.

First make the sighting mechanism as shown at each end of the tube in the diagram, and then construct the scales.

The scales are marked off in convenient regular units of length which must be the same for each scale. The diagram shows how they relate to each other.

Make a notched edge to the height scale that will engage the plumb-line. Now set the distance scale, with its plumb-line attached, at right angles to the height scale and arranged to run freely up and down.

When the hypsometer is used, the measurer stands on level ground in a position where he can sight the top of the tree. He then adjusts the distance scale until the mark showing the correct distance from the tree coincides with the height scale.

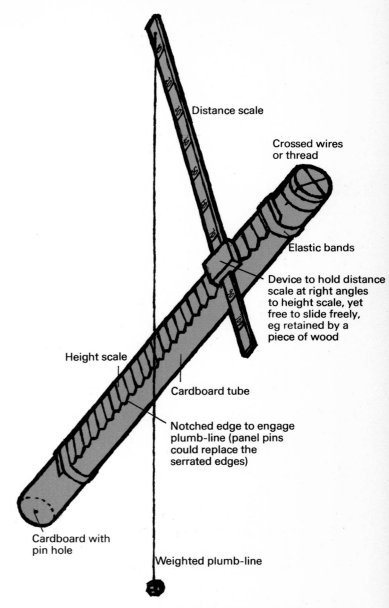

Distance scale

Crossed wires or thread

Elastic bands

Device to hold distance scale at right angles to height scale, yet free to slide freely, eg retained by a piece of wood

Height scale

Cardboard tube

Notched edge to engage plumb-line (panel pins could replace the serrated edges)

Cardboard with pin hole

Weighted plumb-line

The hypsometer, with the plumb-line hanging freely, is used to sight the top of the tree through the pinhole and cross-wires. The hypsometer is then turned until the plumb-line engages a notch on the height scale. This reading, when added to the observer's height, will be the height of the tree.

Making and using callipers

Essentially these are made from three pieces of wood of equal thickness. The base piece is graduated in units appropriate to the size of the trees to be measured.

One 'arm' is permanently fixed to the base piece and the other is arranged to slide freely.

When used the callipers are held at right angles to the trunk with the arms wider apart than the tree's diameter.

The base piece is then pushed towards the tree so that the scale and fixed arm are tight against the trunk. Finally, the free arm is slid along the scale until it touches the trunk and its diameter is then read directly from the scale.

A sturdier model for measuring diameter up to 1 metre is shown in the illustration. Its arms can be removed for easy storage.

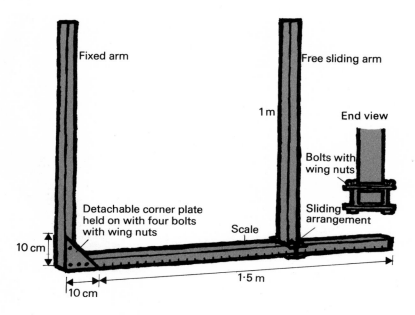

Fixed arm

Free sliding arm

1 m

End view

Bolts with wing nuts

Detachable corner plate held on with four bolts with wing nuts

Scale

Sliding arrangement

10 cm

10 cm

1·5 m

Objectives for children learning science

Guide lines to keep in mind

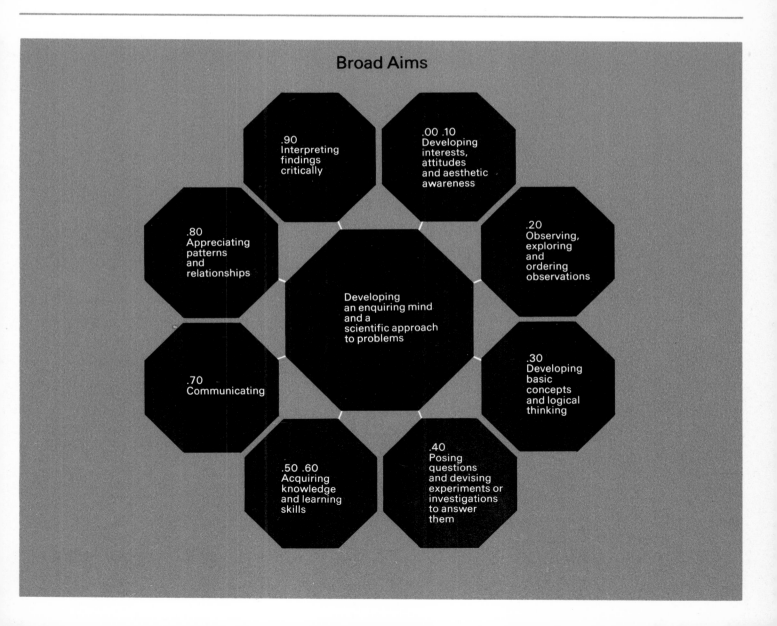

Broad Aims

.90 Interpreting findings critically

.00 .10 Developing interests, attitudes and aesthetic awareness

.80 Appreciating patterns and relationships

.20 Observing, exploring and ordering observations

Developing an enquiring mind and a scientific approach to problems

.70 Communicating

.30 Developing basic concepts and logical thinking

.50 .60 Acquiring knowledge and learning skills

.40 Posing questions and devising experiments or investigations to answer them

What we mean by Stage 1, Stage 2 and Stage 3

Attitudes, interests and aesthetic awareness

.00/.10

Stage 1
Transition from intuition to concrete operations. Infants generally.

The characteristics of thought among infant children differ in important respects from those of children over the age of about seven years. Infant thought has been described as 'intuitive' by Piaget; it is closely associated with physical action and is dominated by immediate observation. Generally, the infant is not able to think about or imagine the consequences of an action unless he has actually carried it out, nor is he yet likely to draw logical conclusions from his experiences. At this early stage the objectives are those concerned with active exploration of the immediate environment and the development of ability to discuss and communicate effectively: they relate to the kind of activities that are appropriate to these very young children, and which form an introduction to ways of exploring and of ordering observations.

1.01 Willingness to ask questions
1.02 Willingness to handle both living and non-living material.
1.03 Sensitivity to the need for giving proper care to living things.
1.04 Enjoyment in using all the senses for exploring and discriminating.
1.05 Willingness to collect material for observation or investigation.

Concrete operations. Early stage.

In this Stage, children are developing the ability to manipulate things mentally. At first this ability is limited to objects and materials that can be manipulated concretely, and even then only in a restricted way. The objectives here are concerned with developing these mental operations through exploration of concrete objects and materials—that is to say, objects and materials which, as physical things, have meaning for the child. Since older children, and even adults, prefer an introduction to new ideas and problems through concrete example and physical exploration, these objectives are suitable for all children, whatever their age, who are being introduced to certain science activities for the first time.

1.06 Desire to find out things for oneself.
1.07 Willing participation in group work.
1.08 Willing compliance with safety regulations in handling tools and equipment.
1.09 Appreciation of the need to learn the meaning of new words and to use them correctly.

Stage 2
Concrete operations. Later stage.

In this Stage, a continuation of what Piaget calls the stage of concrete operations, the mental manipulations are becoming more varied and powerful. The developing ability to handle variables—for example, in dealing with multiple classification—means that problems can be solved in more ordered and quantitative ways than was previously possible. The objectives begin to be more specific to the exploration of the scientific aspects of the environment rather than to general experience, as previously. These objectives are developments of those of Stage 1 and depend on them for a foundation. They are those thought of as being appropriate for all children who have progressed from Stage 1 and not merely for nine- to eleven-year-olds.

2.01 Willingness to co-operate with others in science activities.
2.02 Willingness to observe objectively.
2.03 Appreciation of the reasons for safety regulations.
2.04 Enjoyment in examining ambiguity in the use of words.
2.05 Interest in choosing suitable means of expressing results and observations.
2.06 Willingness to assume responsibility for the proper care of living things.
2.07 Willingness to examine critically the results of their own and others' work.
2.08 Preference for putting ideas to test before accepting or rejecting them.
2.09 Appreciation that approximate methods of comparison may be more appropriate than careful measurements.

Stage 3
Transition to stage of abstract thinking.

This is the Stage in which, for some children, the ability to think about abstractions is developing. When this development is complete their thought is capable of dealing with the possible and hypothetical, and is not tied to the concrete and to the here and now. It may take place between eleven and thirteen for some able children, for some children it may happen later, and for others it may never occur. The objectives of this stage are ones which involve development of ability to use hypothetical reasoning and to separate and combine variables in a systematic way. They are appropriate to those who have achieved most of the Stage 2 objectives and who now show signs of ability to manipulate mentally ideas and propositions.

3.01 Acceptance of responsibility for their own and others' safety in experiments.
3.02 Preference for using words correctly.
3.03 Commitment to the idea of physical cause and effect.
3.04 Recognition of the need to standardise measurements.
3.05 Willingness to examine evidence critically.
3.06 Willingness to consider beforehand the usefulness of the results from a possible experiment.
3.07 Preference for choosing the most appropriate means of expressing results or observations.
3.08 Recognition of the need to acquire new skills.
3.09 Willingness to consider the role of science in everyday life.

Attitudes, interests and aesthetic awareness

.00/.10

Observing, exploring and ordering observations

.20

1.21 Appreciation of the variety of·living things and materials in the environment.
1.22 Awareness of changes which take place as time passes.
1.23 Recognition of common shapes—square, circle, triangle.
1.24 Recognition of regularity in patterns.
1.25 Ability to group things consistently according to chosen or given criteria.

1.11 Awareness that there are various ways of testing out ideas and making observations.
1.12 Interest in comparing and classifying living or non-living things.
1.13 Enjoyment in comparing measurements with estimates.
1.14 Awareness that there are various ways of expressing results and observations.
1.15 Willingness to wait and to keep records in order to observe change in things.
1.16 Enjoyment in exploring the variety of living things in the environment.
1.17 Interest in discussing and comparing the aesthetic qualities of materials.

1.26 Awareness of the structure and form of living things.
1.27 Awareness of change of living things and non-living materials.
1.28 Recognition of the action of force
1.29 Ability to group living and non-living things by observable attributes.
1.29a Ability to distinguish regularity in events and motion.

2.11 Enjoyment in developing methods for solving problems or testing ideas.
2.12 Appreciation of the part that aesthetic qualities of materials play in determining their use.
2.13 Interest in the way discoveries were made in the past.

2.21 Awareness of internal structure in living and non-living things.
2.22 Ability to construct and use keys for identification.
2.23 Recognition of similar and congruent shapes.
2.24 Awareness of symmetry in shapes and structures.
2.25 Ability to classify living things and non-living materials in different ways.
2.26 Ability to visualise objects from different angles and the shape of cross-sections.

3.11 Appreciation of the main principles in the care of living things.
3.12 Willingness to extend methods used in science activities to other fields of experience.

3.21 Appreciation that classification criteria are arbitrary.
3.22 Ability to distinguish observations which are relevant to the solution of a problem from those which are not.
3.23 Ability to estimate the order of magnitude of physical quantities.

Developing basic concepts and logical thinking .30	Posing questions and devising experiments or investigations to answer them .40
Stage 1 Transition from intuition to concrete operations. Infants generally.	**1.31** Awareness of the meaning of words which describe various types of quantity. **1.32** Appreciation that things which are different may have features in common.	**1.41** Ability to find answers to simple problems by investigation. **1.42** Ability to make comparisons in terms of one property or variable.
Concrete operations. Early stage.	**1.33** Ability to predict the effect of certain changes through observation of similar changes. **1.34** Formation of the notions of the horizontal and the vertical. **1.35** Development of concepts of conservation of length and substance. **1.36** Awareness of the meaning of speed and of its relation to distance covered.	**1.43** Appreciation of the need for measurement. **1.44** Awareness that more than one variable may be involved in a particular change.
Stage 2 Concrete operations. Later stage.	**2.31** Appreciation of measurement as division into regular parts and repeated comparison with a unit. **2.32** Appreciation that comparisons can be made indirectly by use of an intermediary. **2.33** Development of concepts of conservation of weight, area and volume. **2.34** Appreciation of weight as a downward force. **2.35** Understanding of the speed, time, distance relation.	**2.41** Ability to frame questions likely to be answered through investigations. **2.42** Ability to investigate variables and to discover effective ones. **2.43** Appreciation of the need to control variables and use controls in investigations. **2.44** Ability to choose and use either arbitrary or standard units of measurement as appropriate. **2.45** Ability to select a suitable degree of approximation and work to it. **2.46** Ability to use representational models for investigating problems or relationships.
Stage 3 Transition to stage of abstract thinking.	**3.31** Familiarity with relationships involving velocity, distance, time, acceleration. **3.32** Ability to separate, exclude or combine variables in approaching problems. **3.33** Ability to formulate hypotheses not dependent upon direct observation. **3.34** Ability to extend reasoning beyond the actual to the possible. **3.35** Ability to distinguish a logically sound proof from others less sound.	**3.41** Attempting to identify the essential steps in approaching a problem scientifically. **3.42** Ability to design experiments with effective controls for testing hypotheses. **3.43** Ability to visualise a hypothetical situation as a useful simplification of actual observations. **3.44** Ability to construct scale models for investigation and to appreciate implications of changing the scale.

1.51 Ability to discriminate between different materials.
1.52 Awareness of the characteristics of living things.
1.53 Awareness of properties which materials can have.
1.54 Ability to use displayed reference material for identifying living and non-living things.

1.55 Familiarity with sources of sound.
1.56 Awareness of sources of heat, light and electricity.
1.57 Knowledge that change can be produced in common substances.
1.58 Appreciation that ability to move or cause movement requires energy.
1.59 Knowledge of differences in properties between and within common groups of materials.

1.61 Appreciation of man's use of other living things and their products.
1.62 Awareness that man's way of life has changed through the ages.
1.63 Skill in manipulating tools and materials.
1.64 Development of techniques for handling living things correctly.
1.65 Ability to use books for supplementing ideas or information.

2.51 Knowledge of conditions which promote changes in living things and non-living materials.
2.52 Familiarity with a wide range of forces and of ways in which they can be changed.
2.53 Knowledge of sources and simple properties of common forms of energy.
2.54 Knowledge of the origins of common materials.
2.55 Awareness of some discoveries and inventions by famous scientists.
2.56 Knowledge of ways to investigate and measure properties of living things and non-living materials.
2.57 Awareness of changes in the design of measuring instruments and tools during man's history.
2.58 Skill in devising and constructing simple apparatus.
2.59 Ability to select relevant information from books or other reference material.

3.51 Knowledge that chemical change results from interaction.
3.52 Knowledge that energy can be stored and converted in various ways.
3.53 Awareness of the universal nature of gravity.
3.54 Knowledge of the main constituents and variations in the composition of soil and of the earth.
3.55 Knowledge that properties of matter can be explained by reference to its particulate nature.
3.56 Knowledge of certain properties of heat, light, sound, electrical, mechanical and chemical energy.
3.57 Knowledge of a wide range of living organisms.
3.58 Development of the concept of an internal environment.
3.59 Knowledge of the nature and variations in basic life processes.

3.61 Appreciation of levels of organisation in living things.
3.62 Appreciation of the significance of the work and ideas of some famous scientists.
3.63 Ability to apply relevant knowledge without help of contextual cues.
3.64 Ability to use scientific equipment and instruments for extending the range of human senses.

Communicating	Appreciating patterns and relationships
.70	**.80**

Stage 1
Transition from
intuition to
concrete
operations.
Infants
generally.

1.71 Ability to use new words appropriately.
1.72 Ability to record events in their sequences.
1.73 Ability to discuss and record impressions of living and non-living things in the environment.
1.74 Ability to use representational symbols for recording information on charts or block graphs.

1.81 Awareness of cause-effect relationships.

**Concrete
operations.
Early stage.**

1.75 Ability to tabulate information and use tables.
1.76 Familiarity with names of living things and non-living materials.
1.77 Ability to record impressions by making models, painting or drawing.

1.82 Development of a concept of environment.
1.83 Formation of a broad idea of variation in living things.
1.84 Awareness of seasonal changes in living things.
1.85 Awareness of differences in physical conditions between different parts of the Earth.

Stage 2
Concrete
operations.
Later stage.

2.71 Ability to use non-representational symbols in plans, charts, etc.
2.72 Ability to interpret observations in terms of trends and rates of change.
2.73 Ability to use histograms and other simple graphical forms for communicating data.
2.74 Ability to construct models as a means of recording observations.

2.81 Awareness of sequences of change in natural phenomena.
2.82 Awareness of structure-function relationship in parts of living things.
2.83 Appreciation of interdependence among living things.
2.84 Awareness of the impact of man's activities on other living things.
2.85 Awareness of the changes in the physical environment brought about by man's activity.
2.86 Appreciation of the relationships of parts and wholes.

Stage 3
Transition to
stage of
abstract
thinking.

3.71 Ability to select the graphical form most appropriate to the information being recorded.
3.72 Ability to use three-dimensional models or graphs for recording results.
3.73 Ability to deduce information from graphs: from gradient, area, intercept.
3.74 Ability to use analogies to explain scientific ideas and theories.

3.81 Recognition that the ratio of volume to surface area is significant.
3.82 Appreciation of the scale of the universe.
3.83 Understanding of the nature and significance of changes in living and non-living things.
3.84 Recognition that energy has many forms and is conserved when it is changed from one form to another.
3.85 Recognition of man's impact on living things—conservation, change, control.
3.86 Appreciation of the social implications of man's changing use of materials, historical and contemporary.
3.87 Appreciation of the social implications of research in science.
3.88 Appreciation of the role of science in the changing pattern of provision for human needs.

Interpreting findings critically

.90

1.91 Awareness that the apparent size, shape and relationships of things depend on the position of the observer.

1.92 Appreciation that properties of materials influence their use.

2.91 Appreciation of adaptation to environment.
2.92 Appreciation of how the form and structure of materials relate to their function and properties.
2.93 Awareness that many factors need to be considered when choosing a material for a particular use.
2.94 Recognition of the role of chance in making measurements and experiments.

3.91 Ability to draw from observations conclusions that are unbiased by preconception.
3.92 Willingness to accept factual evidence despite perceptual contradictions.
3.93 Awareness that the degree of accuracy of measurements has to be taken into account when results are interpreted.
3.94 Awareness that unstated assumptions can affect conclusions drawn from argument or experimental results.
3.95 Appreciation of the need to integrate findings into a simplifying generalisation.
3.96 Willingness to check that conclusions are consistent with further evidence.

These Stages we have chosen conform to modern ideas about children's learning. They conveniently describe for us the mental development of children between the ages of five and thirteen years, but it must be remembered that ALTHOUGH CHILDREN GO THROUGH THESE STAGES IN THE SAME ORDER THEY DO NOT GO THROUGH THEM AT THE SAME RATES.
SOME children achieve the later Stages at an early age.
SOME loiter in the early Stages for quite a time.
SOME never have the mental ability to develop to the later Stages.
ALL appear to be ragged in their movement from one Stage to another.
Our Stages, then, are not tied to chronological age, so in any one class of children there will be, almost certainly, some children at differing Stages of mental development.

Index

Illustration acknowledgements:

The publishers gratefully acknowledge the help given by the
following in supplying photographs on the pages indicated:

Aerofilms Limited, 31 bottom
Heather Angel, 12, 41, 51, 53, 54, 55
Forestry Commission, 57, 64
By courtesy of Fyffes group, 22
Greater London Council, 31 top right
M Nimmo, 27 left, 32 top right
Southern Tree Surgeons, 30
South West Picture Agency, 16

All other photographs by James Wright

Line drawings by The Garden Studio: Anna Barnard

Labelling and flow charts by GWA Design Consultants

Cover design by Peter Gauld